RIPPLES

TRAGEDY TO TRIUMPH

BY

DWAIN HARRIS

ISBN:

978-969-53-9239-3 (E-book)

978-969-53-9240-9 (Paperback)

978-969-53-9241-6 (Hardcover)

Table of Contents

(Page intentionally left blank)

DEDICATION

When we think of Collin's legacy, our first thoughts are of Valley Grove Baptist Church in Stephenville, Texas. As the congregation embraced him, they also honored him by establishing the "Friends of Collin" class. It is an outreach program to seek out and integrate individuals, often overlooked because of various disabilities, into the congregation. The church and "Friends of Collin" class, directed by Debbie Knipstein since inception, has made life better for many individuals and their families for about 40 years in the same manner as they made life better for Collin and our family.

ABOUT THE AUTHOR

Ripples was compiled from memories and records of the past 55 years. My wife, Becky, and I had contemplated writing something along the lines of Ripples for years, to immortalize, in writing, the journey of our beloved son, Collin.

In our mid-seventies, while our minds are still clear, I decided to begin the book. The choices were to start writing or stop thinking about it. I couldn't convince myself to not write it. After many months of sporadically developing the story, Becky realized she had to get involved if the book were to be meaningfully completed. She added to, edited, and inserted additional details, not in her chosen style, but mine.

Though we are equally complicit, Becky is determined that I be recognized as the author. "We" wrote Ripples together and "I'm" the author. That doesn't seem right, but that is how she wants it.

We had to write Ripples for ourselves. It has been beneficial to us. We hope it can be beneficial to others as well.

PREFACE

RIPPLES is a story based on the life of our Special first child, Collin. The narrative starts before his birth and continues through the time of his death and beyond, focusing primarily on Collin's journey through life and the influences he has had on many others. The **MIRACULOUS ENDING** of this story will definitely **AFFECT** and is almost certain to **SURPRISE** you.

When a pebble splashes into a pond, ripples are created that move in all directions. Those ripples are interesting to watch as they swell and expand. Eventually they end and do not change history. But there are single events in life with enormous ripples that do change history for individuals, groups, and multitudes that reach well beyond all our imaginations. Ripples can be devastating or enormously positive. They can cement or alter perspectives and paths in the blink of an eye.

Collin's birth was an event that profoundly affected our family, friends, and many others in many circumstances and relationships. Who can know how far the effects of that event five decades ago may travel? I am convinced the influences are still being felt. This one event, initially perceived as devastating, continues as a tremendous positive for our family and many others touched (directly or indirectly) by it.

Collin lived a little over 32 ½ years. Unknown to him, he had a tremendous effect on the lives of many, including some who never knew or heard of him. His story is unique. It took unexpected turns, positive and negative, and changed the course of history for many people. Once a path in life is altered, everything is different than it would have been. New paths forge changes that grow at geometric rates. Volumes could be written about the perceived and unperceived changes created by the birth of Collin. Ripples, the story, will be restrained by the limited narrative of his travels through life, including family path changes, and his most conspicuous ripples.

Becky and I could not have been more blessed than to have traveled together on a journey with Collin, his sisters, Deanne and Amy, and our precious and growing extended families. Our family dealt with Collin's situation as we thought best, as would every other loving family. Any insights into how our decisions were made regarding our journey with Collin are incidental to telling his story.

CHAPTER ONE
THE BEGINNING

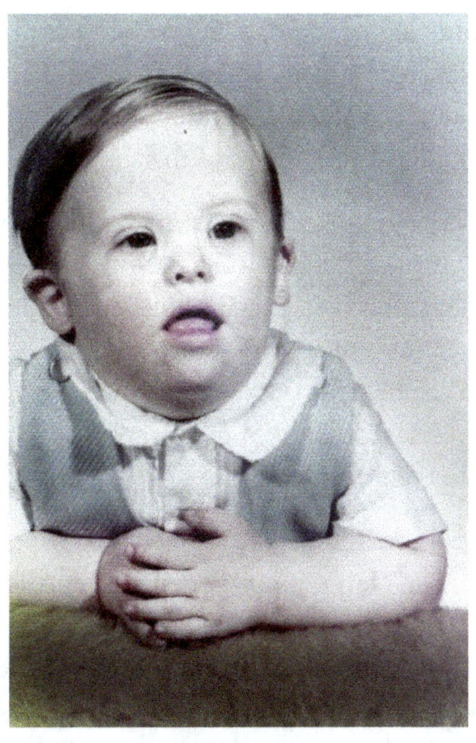

Collin's story began at Texas Tech University in Lubbock, Texas, well before he was born. On December 6, 1968, I attended the Carol of Lights celebration that kicks off the Christmas season on campus. It was a brisk, snowy evening full of cheer as the lights were turned on campus-wide. A dance followed at the Student Union building. There was a large crowd with a great band, and it was already rocking when I arrived.

After a couple of songs, I spotted someone who really impressed me. She was beautiful and I couldn't wait to meet her. Unfortunately, she was not impressed with me at all. I was surprised to get turned down when I asked her for a dance, but it happened. Ouch! I just had to become acquainted with her before she left. This might be the only opportunity to meet her. Having already been rejected and with my ego bruised, there was nothing to lose by trying again.

So, I polished up my approach as much as I knew how and asked again. Luckily, Becky consented to a dance. It turned out that she was much nicer than I could have imagined, and she could tolerate me for a second dance. The rest is history. We were married on December 20, 1969. I discovered that she was not only the love of my life, but an anchor for the long haul, regardless of the state of the seas.

After a brief honeymoon, Becky and I settled into a "teacherage" in Afton, Texas, across the road from the rural school from which I graduated four years previously, one of eleven seniors. I taught math, drove a school bus during the school days, and farmed the remainder of the time. From the beginning, we had planned to have at least three children, so we were excited out of our minds when the time came for the birth of our first child.

Our home was more than an hour from the hospital at the time of Collin's birth, so when labor pains began in the early morning hours of April 6, 1971, we left immediately and headed to West Texas Hospital in Lubbock. One of the nurses in the ER suggested we go home, that Becky was most likely experiencing false labor. As we were waiting to be discharged, another nurse smiled at Becky and said, "Honey, don't you worry, that baby is coming today." The nurse called the obstetrician, and he summoned Becky to his office, which was a few floors above the hospital.

As she stepped from the elevator, she experienced what was the first pain of intense labor and was quickly taken back downstairs to the hospital. Becky described an eerie quietness that descended in the delivery room immediately after our baby was delivered, the silence broken only by our newborn's cry and the obstetrician announcing the baby was a boy. As Becky was anxiously anticipating holding our son, she had only a glimpse of his back before he was whisked away. Before she could protest, she was sedated and hours passed as she slept, unaware that we were about to embark on a much different journey than the one we had so joyously anticipated.

"PERFECT" … was the only way to describe the first sight of my newborn son. NO DOUBT he would be a MAN AMONG MEN…loved by women, envied by men, feared yet respected by his enemies. All that was obvious at first glance! WOW!! While viewing Collin through the nursery window the pediatrician came by to report on Collin's first checkup. I was anxious to hear his confirmation of what I already knew.

The only word that I fully remember from that report was "Mongoloid." Although I did not know what Mongoloid, an outdated term for Down Syndrome, fully meant, I understood that something was terribly wrong and to expect developmental issues. I thought my head would explode. There were so many thoughts going through my mind simultaneously, that it was almost impossible to sort them out.

Surely, the doctor was wrong and enjoyed being the bearer of bad news ... insane but true reaction. How could the pediatrician be so heartless to tell us something like this? All of this, while in my heart of hearts, I knew better. The pediatrician did exactly as he was supposed to do.

The news was devastating and something that only happened to other folks. NOT US!! How was I going to tell Becky? To see disappointment in her eyes would be unbearable. How could I tell the family who would not only be heartbroken over the news but worried over Becky and me as well? The sedative Becky was given had presumably been administered to allow her to rest before being confronted with the shocking revelation that was soon to follow. What an awakening she had coming!

Still groggy from the sedative, Becky awoke much later to the muffled sound of my voice in the hallway, conversing with someone whose voice she did not recognize. Hearing the tension in my voice, she anxiously called out to me, sensing my distress. She said she felt certain the effects of the medication had clouded her thinking, and surely all was well with our newborn son. She wondered, had some family member had an accident as they traveled to welcome the latest addition? As I approached Becky's hospital bed, my somber expression confirmed her worst fear as she braced for disturbing news. As I uttered the word, "Mongoloid," she became even more anxious to see our new son.

After we had a few minutes to try and process the doctor's report, a nurse brought our son to us. The feeling of love and responsibility was overwhelming as he curled his tiny fingers around Becky's. We had already decided that if the baby was a boy, we would name him Collin Dwain. Gently touching his soft little ears and seeing the epicanthic folds in the corners of his eyes, we understood the doctor's diagnosis, but as we looked into those beautiful blue eyes, we knew that regardless of the final test results, together Becky and I would move heaven and earth for Collin!

Collin was the 11th addition to Becky's parents' grandchildren. As their family expanded, her parents instilled the importance of familial support. The Smiths had an expression for how they dealt with life's unexpected trouble. They "circle the wagons." As soon as the news spread about Collin, many of Becky's family from South Texas, as well as my relatives nearby, headed to West Texas Hospital. Becky's mama had planned to spend a few days helping us at our home, as was her custom with the birth of her grandchildren.

Becky's daddy's first visit to West Texas Hospital was back in the 1940s when his dad had a car accident nearby and suffered a fatal injury. Becky said, "My Daddy was usually stoic in the face of trouble, but as we stood side by side looking through the nursery window, a tear trickled down his cheek, the only tear I had ever seen on his face. He had dealt with tragedy in his younger years and recognized the challenges ahead for two young parents who had never experienced adversity."

Becky said, "My daddy's reaction reinforced for me that raising a child with disabilities could be a daunting task." The reality of the challenges ahead was confirmed a few days later when a chromosomal test verified the presence of an extra chromosome trisomy 21, the most common type of Down Syndrome.

My Becky is a "ROCK" … She was shocked, devastated, and hurt, but not the least bit deterred. I remember the first time my parents visited the hospital. Becky's words to them were "I'll be back next year." From the first second of his life, Collin had unconditional and unlimited love, with an even greater sense of responsibility from us as parents as well as a multitude of family and others. Devastated for moments only, we could not have been more proud parents.

We loved the obstetrician. I will never forget our conversation with him shortly after Collin's birth. We were both shooting questions at him that no mortal could possibly answer. He interrupted us and said this. Paraphrasing, "Don't be crossing bridges until you get to them. You are going to have bridges to cross, but you don't yet know what they will be". Then he asked us, "Do you believe in the Bible?"

Our answer was a firm yes. Then he said, "Read Romans 8:28. It will help you if you believe it". We were familiar with that verse but read it again with special attention. It reads "And we know that all things work together for good to them that love God, to them who are the called according to his purpose". Although that scripture is difficult to understand in all circumstances, Becky and I firmly believe in those words. They have not let us down yet. We trust they never will. Certainly, some will interpret that scripture differently.

We understood that the plans we had in store for the new arrival would have to be altered. We didn't know how to begin to plan, but we were confident we could make the adjustments. From a young age, I remember being taught the value of family unity and pulling together. A particular story was repeated by my dad many times as an example. The story made sense then and it still does.

My dad had three sisters. His father handed one of the children a stick and said, "Break it." The stick was easily broken. Then he bound four sticks together and said, "Break this." The bundle didn't break.

The point was obvious. This important principle has endured through generations with both of our families. It has helped us immensely through Collin's difficulties and other life trials. We never doubted we could handle what was to come, because we were going to pull together.

CHAPTER TWO
EARLY YEARS

Soon after we arrived home from the hospital, a few friends and family, stopped by with casseroles, cakes, and cookies. An older couple who shared our Christian views offered heartwarming words of encouragement. Becky thoroughly enjoyed the visit of a neighbor who had a baby of her own and understood the challenges of caring for a newborn. She amused us with humorous accounts of sleep interrupted by a fussy baby who was unable to understand the merits of a schedule for sleep.

We hosted get-togethers and attended local gatherings just as we had before our family addition. We played cards and dominoes as Collin slept nearby just as before we became parents. Our lives had changed dramatically, as it does with any couple with a newborn, yet relationships with friends remained constant. One evening we attended a local social event, encountering people we had not seen since Collin's birth.

The usual chatter stopped abruptly when we walked in the door. As anxious glances were exchanged, their discomfort was palpable as they struggled to think of appropriate conversations. They didn't want to say the wrong thing. We made sure they were comfortable as Collin was passed from one friend to another. Caring for Collin as an infant was just like caring for any other infant.

Although we expected Collin to develop at a slower pace, we were surprised and encouraged when he turned over unassisted at only a few weeks of age, far earlier than most. He smiled, laughed, sat alone, and crawled, all within the average time frame for any child. His pediatrician suggested that his progress might indicate a higher functioning level than we initially anticipated. Unfortunately, those developmental phases did not continue at the pace hoped for. He was about seventeen months old when he began to walk. It was easy to connect with him and keep his attention, much the same as any child, but the development pace slowed considerably as time passed.

The first summer after Collin was born, I took a course titled "Exceptional Children," which included a broad range of discussions concerning intellectual disabilities, including what was referred to until the 2000s as "profound mental retardation," currently more likely categorized as acute intellectual disability. We wanted to know as much as we could about the range of expectations. Although the course didn't answer specific questions about "how to," it did bring some valuable insights. One of those insights is that society generally lacks understanding of those with acute intellectual disabilities. Because of societal misunderstandings, many intellectually disabled individuals are often unintentionally subjected to damaging interactions with some people.

Additionally, the acutely intellectually challenged may not have an ego in the same sense most of us do. That can be helpful to them. For example, a slow learner who realizes he cannot keep up with his peers regardless of how hard he tries, unbeknown to others, sometimes has a difficult time coping in life. His ego can sometimes be perpetually and hurtfully damaged. What is more important day to day than how one feels about self? Time revealed Collin apparently felt no peer pressure to compete with or measure up to anybody. That was a good thing.

Thoughts of whether we should have other children entered our minds. Our reasoning was unique to us as it would be for any other couple. Having grown up with four siblings, Becky's home life was never dull, often challenging, but always filled with love. After Collin's birth, Becky was anxious to ensure he had a similar experience. Parents of one child with trisomy 21 have a very low probability of having another child with the same condition. With the understanding that any pregnancy has risks, we kept to our plan to have other children.

Becky did as she said she would. Actually, she was a month late. She said next year, but thirteen months after Collin's birth, we had a new addition; our baby girl, Deanne, a perfect redheaded beauty. When Collin started walking, Deanne was already crawling, and together they were exploring and getting into all sorts of mischief. Although Collin's initial development was similar to Deanne's, he progressed at an increasingly slower rate as time passed.

Learning to drink from a glass was difficult for him. He wanted to bite rather than sip. We spoon-fed him water or offered him a sippy cup until he was two years old. On one occasion, I was sitting on a couch holding a glass of tea about knee level, when Collin crawled up, grabbed the glass suddenly, and bit the side out of it. The glass broke into pieces. Luckily it didn't shatter. We retrieved all the pieces from his mouth and he was fine.

Biscuits were one of Collin's favorites. He loved to both eat and throw them. For whatever reason, Collin decided that to take a bite from the biscuit and throw what was left across the room was the thing to do. It brought him great pleasure! Discipline him for wasting biscuits? Nah! The answer was to make plenty of biscuits and clean up the mess. He was having FUN! Nothing wrong with that.

We eventually moved to Abernathy Texas in the summer of 1973, where I continued to teach school while still working ninety miles away at the farm. My aunt and uncle lived nearby and were always available to keep the kids for a few hours to give us a break. Their grandchildren were happy to entertain Collin, attempting to share their toys with him. The little boys had no previous interaction with a mentally challenged child who sat mesmerized by the specks of dust illuminated by a shaft of light from the window.

They sat in wonder as he lay propped on his elbows, tirelessly barely touching the end of a soft cotton string to the floor, ignoring their attempts to interest him in their trucks and action figures. Being forced to watch the dangling string long enough could qualify as torture. Interrogation agencies could have gleaned any information needed by forcing the interrogee to watch him dangle that string! Collin would have entertained himself and the subject would have spilled his guts without physical harm. That would have been a win-win.

The following February, we had a new addition to our family. Our lovely precocious daughter, Amy, joined our happy clan. So here we were with three children born between April 1971 and February 1974, and one of them was Collin. Fortunately, this was before seat belt and child safety requirements. We had a port-a-crib, which is a baby bed with two legs on the floorboard and the other side of the bed supported by the car seat. One could probably be jailed these days for using one of those. Traveling with these three little ones was very interesting.

Because Collin did everything last, there were three in diapers for a while. Sometimes there were two of the kids in the back and one in mom's lap in the front. Just as often there were three in the back with mom leaning over the seat, rear in the windshield, trying to sort out the unsortable. There was NO WAY I was turning loose of the steering wheel. Survival instincts kicked in and I did all the driving. The children seemed to need Mom more than me anyway. Whether we made a short trip to Granny's house or a long trip to Grandma's, the port-a crib was in play.

Collin's lack of mental capabilities soon became more and more apparent. Some doubted he could ever be toilet trained, but eventually with Mama's persistence and Granny's help, he succeeded. You have not begun to have fun until you travel ten hours with someone in the car who will not use a public restroom. Nope, Collin wouldn't go until he got to Grandma's house. No substitutes. The last few hours, taking required stops, and Collin getting more tense by the minute, are still burned into our brains.

We made a few of those trips and picked up some speeding tickets along the way. We should have asked for a police escort. However, Collin did get us out of at least one ticket. One night, while the good officer was checking to see what was in the car, Collin showed him exactly what he could do while he was about to explode. In his state of discomfort, he just couldn't see any reason to be stopped on the side of the road, speaking with someone wearing a hat and shining a flashlight on him. The officer was quite willing to wave us on.

Collin loved being at his grandparents' house. We didn't say "no" enough. Grandparents said no even less, and they were always ready with something new to introduce to the kids. I will never forget stopping at a department store in Alice Texas on the way to Grandma and Grandaddy's house near Harlingen. While Becky and the girls were shopping for last-minute Christmas gifts, Collin and I discovered an escalator. I thought he might enjoy the experience of riding on it. He loved it!

Imagine riding a roller coaster with the kids screaming and wildly waving their arms with every drop and turn. Collin did exactly that while "slowly" riding up and down the escalator… MANY round trips. Think about it. Thankfully we were among strangers. This was a special Christmas outing for Collin. We could give quite a few folks something to talk about during Christmas festivities, and nobody would get hurt.

The worst that could happen would be to get thrown out. It was a no-brainer. We went all in. Everybody heard the commotion. I'm fairly certain it shortened Becky's decision-making time. Whatever she had picked up was good enough for who it was for. AND…nobody in the store said anything nasty to us. That may have been a trifecta. Though well earned, we didn't get thrown out or even threatened.

Christmas at Grandma's! How Collin loved being surrounded by a houseful of cousins, entertaining them with his pie pan spinning. At a very young age, Collin could prop on his elbows and spin a pie pan like a top. He would watch it spin down with his nose almost touching the pan until it settled on the floor. He repeated the process over and over and over…. and over…. Much to their consternation, none of his cousins could emulate his skill.

He loved having an audience and didn't want anyone to miss the fun. Becky's brother, Clifford, was dozing on the couch one afternoon. Collin dashed by, not stopping, to tap him on the head. Christmas celebrations were no time for sleeping! As the room filled with laughter, Collin realized he had discovered a new way to connect with and entertain his audience.

My brother, Gene, and dad, Pa, were frequent recipients of these little love taps as well. Later as my dad's health declined, Collin would approach him slowly, gently touching his head. Somehow, he knew….

Becky's sister, Jessica, presented him with a cuddly musical bear one Christmas. He loved hugging the soft furry bear while listening to Christmas music year-round. We were always ready with new batteries to ensure the bear survived until the following Christmas when Aunt Jessica would present him with a new one. Christmas in July seemed a little strange to us, but Collin never tired of the bears and their music.

His cousin, Michelle, introduced him to sign language, teaching him the sign for "smile." He would sit with her in his favorite chair at Grandma's, beaming while she whispered secrets in his ear. Shared secrets and signing "smile" were a source of pleasure for him that he enjoyed his entire life, a tradition carried on by both Deanne and Amy as well as Michelle.

Hair fascinated Collin. He loved to lightly touch and pat hair with the back of his hand, especially women's hair. It was better if the lady had just left the hair salon. Becky's brother-in-law Steve said, "Back when I had a full head of red hair, I was also the recipient of his patting. He had the most tender touch imaginable, and it had to be a true sign of affection." But at times, he would reach out and touch a stranger's hair. We did our best to protect the unsuspecting.

If you wanted to know where all the light switches in the house were, follow Collin. One of his first chores in any house was to discover all the light switches and turn them on and off a few times. He especially enjoyed turning them all on in the very early morning hours just after everyone had finally gotten sound asleep. If we wanted the girls, or Becky's college sister, to get out of bed, we put Collin in the bed with them or gave him a tiny bit of water in a glass. Either way, they were getting up.

CHAPTER THREE
THE FARM

In 1976 when Collin was five, we relocated to the farm, leaving the teaching job to focus totally on farming and the cattle operation. Deanne and Amy were thrilled at the prospect of living on the farm near their grandparents, The house was also near the home of my brother Gene, his wife Elaine, and their three children, Randall, Melissa, and Kristi. These three kids were close in age to our three. Those six kids spent a tremendous amount of time together. Collin was generally involved in whatever the others were doing, and his cousins and sisters all made allowances from a very young age, as he was always welcome to participate. Regardless of whether a birthday celebration was for him, a cousin, or a sister, he assumed it was his birthday, which was fine with all the participants.

He had not mastered the art of blowing out candles, preferring to "snuff" them out. Of course, this would not be acceptable to anybody. Since Collin intended to extinguish the candles (for "his" birthday party), a piece of cake was set aside with a candle for Collin to snuff out while the others were doing their candle thing. His cousins singing "Happy Birthday" was a treat, but what really made him happy was listening to Doug Kershaw play his Cajun fiddle. Collin performed his signature dance, bouncing his little behind almost to the floor to the sounds of Kershaw belting out "Diggy Liggy Lo." He had a captive audience for those performances!

Some of our fondest memories with siblings, cousins, friends, and family involve Collin at the center of attention, laughing his head off. He observed a lot and sometimes misinterpreted some of the applications of what he saw. Collin was in the living room while we were watching boxing on TV at Granny and Pa's house. Granny took Collin to the kitchen sink to help her with the dishes. What do you suppose he did when she put the rubber gloves on his hands? Of course, he started swinging. Those guys on TV had gloves. They were swinging, so that was the next step.

Early in Collin's life, Becky's sister Jessica advised us to laugh at the things he did. As she said, "We laugh at ourselves and each other when one of us does something goofy, why not Collin, too?" We embraced that idea. In some way that helped normalize the situation. Believe me, he gave us a lot to laugh about, often laughing the loudest. He loved being the center of attention and continued entertaining us with his antics throughout his life. No need to bore you with too many episodes, but trust me, there were exciting, strange, and happy times in our household.

Living on the farm meant all of us were able to spend most days together. Quite often, Becky and the kids would bring lunch to me in the field, workshop, or corral. The kids all loved feeding the cows and sometimes getting to touch them. The girls and I have very fond memories of installing about three miles of a plastic pipe water line. It connected to a strong water well with an electric pump to replace the water supplied by two windmills, which were prone to need repair at the most inconvenient times. At six and eight years of age, the girls would take the one-inch diameter plastic pipes from a low trailer and line them up next to the ditch I had just dug with a tractor and blade.

The pipe sections were 20 feet long but very light. One on each end could easily handle the pipe. I would glue the pipe sections together while they were lining up the next section of pipe. Then the girls and I would move the connected pipes into the ditch. When the pipes were situated properly, I would fill in the ditch with the blade. Deanne and Amy were very helpful and loved every minute of it. The part of this story the girls always mention is when I plowed into a wasp nest in the ground. Some of the wasps flew up Amy's pants legs. Fortunately, she didn't get stung, but she came out of those pants in a hurry! Collin would not have been helpful, but I'm sorry he missed the wasp episode. He would have loved it.

We were in a remote area in a much different era. Though unacceptable now, I had each of our children, including Collin, sitting in my lap at times with their hands on the wheel, while driving. They all "drove" many a mile sitting in my lap. A child can sense when dad is using his thumbs to keep control of the wheel. They all enjoyed sitting in my lap driving, but none liked it when I prevented them from spinning the wheel. They wanted full control, even as toddlers.

Collin did not have the natural fears most of us do. Walking by a fence with a vicious barking dog makes many of us naturally shy away …NOT COLLIN. If anything, he might get closer. We had rattlesnakes at the farm. I was paranoid about the children getting bit. So, I built a snake-proof solid fence with no gates, accessible only through the kitchen door so that the kids could play in the backyard without risk. The girls would have known to run from a snake. For certain, Collin would have wanted to pick up the rattling creature. The fence would have been built for the girls alone, but it was an absolute requirement for Collin's safety.

One snowy week all five of us had the flu, on the brink of "stir-crazy." After a few days, Collin made an executive decision. He wanted to go somewhere, anywhere! He grabbed his shoes and headed to the door. He was ending this isolation. Time to "get the hell out of Dodge!" He couldn't talk, but he could absolutely communicate.

Although Collin immensely enjoyed being with his grandparents, he didn't want to miss any outings. There were a few occasions that necessitated leaving him with my parents for a few hours for various reasons. After this had happened a few times, we drove up to Granny's house to let Collin out. NO WAY he was going to get left out of something again. He wouldn't get out of the car. We all had to go inside and Granny had to get him cranked up in an activity of some kind before anybody was leaving without him.

One of Granny's favorite games was to go into a bedroom with Collin, yell "get outta there" and run out of the room. Collin would join her full-heartedly running and laughing. He usually slammed the door, while attempting to mimic her sounds. Yeah, he could have been a politician. He could be bribed. The occasions of leaving Collin behind were few and far between; Collin was generally with us wherever we went, except on very rare occasions, e.g. weddings and funerals. There are times when raucous laughter, etc. would not be appropriate.

Collin became addicted to Captain Crunch cereal. TOTALLY HOOKED. He decided it was his life's mission to eat Captain Crunch cereal all day long. I would sit him on my shoulders and walk through the house, making a big deal about ducking his head going through doorways. When asked if he wanted to duck his head, Collin would back up to me with outstretched arms to take a ride through the house. The Point…after Collin had become "addicted," we had to wean him "cold turkey." Becky placed the cereal box high enough in the cabinet that he couldn't reach it, even by scooting up a chair. The first time he saw me after the cereal was out of range, Collin backed up to me for his ride. On my shoulders, he grabbed me by the hair and reined me like a horse to the cabinet door with the cereal. The boy was mentally challenged, but he was no dummy.

One afternoon as Becky and Collin were on a grocery run, Collin's unusual behavior attracted the attention of a young boy. He had wandered an aisle over from his mother. Unable to suppress his curiosity, he innocently asked, "Is he blind?" Although his mom was within hearing distance of his question, she remained just out of sight. Becky gave the child a brief answer, hoping a positive experience with

Collin might help him in a future encounter with a child with physical or mental challenges.

When encountering Collin for the first time, most small children exhibited an innocent inquisitiveness. Collin was oblivious to these incidents, and therefore never troubled by them. I remember an especially funny event while in a shopping mall. A young child was pointing out Collin to his mom. Mom was frantically and unsuccessfully trying to distract her youngster without attracting our attention. It was only seconds, but hilarious. We made certain she knew we weren't bothered at all and had a good laugh with her. I have to admit some of our funniest jokes have been at Collin's expense. You get a laugh where you can.

When Amy was about 5 years old, she was offended by a teenage boy's snickering, his gaze fixed on Collin. Even at her young age, she realized the teen was old enough to know better, and he quickly looked away when she shamed him with a cold, hard stare. These were isolated incidents, but at a young age, neither Deanne nor Amy ever felt shame or embarrassment regarding Collin. In her words, Amy remembers "feeling proud" when introducing her brother to her first-grade classmates.

CHAPTER FOUR
MONUMENTAL MOVE

We were farmers in a small community 30 miles from a grocery store. Collin was nine years old and the local schools were too small to provide a program for a child with his limitations and issues. I think they would have been required to provide something, but that wouldn't have been fair to the school or Collin. We had been trying to decide what to do for a few years and we were already late providing a structured program for him. His needs required a major decision by Becky and me.

We realized a larger community would be more likely to have appropriate accommodations for special needs children of his estimated mental age level of 17-18 months and IQ around 19. Although we knew the move would be disruptive, the decision to move was certain. Where we would move to, when we would move, and how we could accomplish the transition were difficult decisions. Deanne and Amy's needs were equally included in the calculus of what our actions might be.

Becky and I weighed our options, researched programs, and concluded that Stephenville Texas checked more boxes than any other location, even though it was over 200 miles away from my business. Loading up and driving off is still etched in my mind. We had lived only a few hundred yards from my parents for years. The children were strongly attached to our home and their local grandparents and other extended family living nearby. Driving away from that daily contact was tough for everyone. Even the dog knew something was up. He chased the U-Haul as we drove away. However, during the summer months, we were all back at the farm.

We arrived in Stephenville in the summer of 1980, excited and hopeful. We rented a house and looked forward to enrolling the children in school. Stephenville ISD had an exemplary elementary school for Deanne and Amy and a highly rated program for children with special needs for Collin, which included adaptive P.E. and music therapy.

Settling in included exploring our new community. Driving through the outskirts of town, we noticed a small chapel, Valley Grove Baptist Church. The banner out front announced the schedule for Vacation Bible School the following week, which we thought would be a good opportunity for the kids to meet other children. We received a warm welcome when we drove into the parking lot of the church a few days later.

Each day of that week as we arrived to deposit the girls for VBS, we continued to meet other church members, and realized we had found our church "home." Sunday mornings, we were greeted at the door with a handshake, which quickly changed to hugs as we developed strong bonds with sweet people who became close friends. Some of the older couples treated our kids as though they were their grandchildren, easing the pain of separation from their grandparents.

Our pastor, C.O. Herchenhahn, was one of the best of the best pastors as well as a great speaker and close personal friend. His words of wisdom offered strength and counsel. Though he has passed, we still remember his advice and leadership. C.O., Charlotte, and their children became dear lifelong friends.

We were encouraged to bring Collin and the girls to Sunday School before church, but we expressed concern that Collin would be disruptive to the children's group. We were assured he would be welcome in the children's class, but when we declined, he was invited to accompany us to the adult group, and eventually, we acquiesced. Initially, Collin was quiet.

After a time, he grew restless, making noises and interrupting the flow of discussion. The adults' smiles soon gave way to chuckles, and realizing he was the source of their amusement, Collin became creative in his attempts to entertain. Class dismissed! We thanked them profusely for their willingness to include Collin but decided not to further disrupt future meetings.

A few weeks later, Valley Grove Baptist Church designated a classroom for Collin, and a special education teacher in public school, Debbie, volunteered to serve as the teacher. Eventually, the church decided to convert two small classrooms into one larger room for Collin. I stated to one of the leaders that we didn't expect special treatment and the accommodation wasn't necessary. His reply, paraphrasing, "We are not accommodating Collin. He has done more for this church than anyone ever has. The church is being accommodated." The Church saw this TRUTH, penned by John Bradford, "There but for the Grace of God, go I."

I must admit that Arthur, one of the church members of Valley Grove taught Collin a "cuss word." Arthur and his wife Beverly stayed with Collin for a few hours one afternoon. When we returned, Arthur proudly announced, "I taught ole' Collin a cuss word." He said "Collin, what's your cuss word?" With a giant grin, Collin strongly whacked his chest with his fist! Although he couldn't talk, he could show someone his word. Collin was about ten or eleven years old at the time. He never forgot and was always ready to show you his "cuss word." Leave it to an active church member, with the cleanest language ever, to corrupt our son's language within only a few hours. I suppose that was one of the accommodations.

Valley Grove continued their mission by finding ways to recruit, embrace, and provide for a group of people often ignored and underserved in the community. We were humbled when the "Friends of Collin" class was created and designed to serve those with Special Needs and integrate them into the congregation. The following summer, the church provided Vacation Bible School for mentally challenged children and young adults.

Years later after we left Stephenville, the class continued to grow, and Debbie, the sweet special education teacher continued in her role, posting the following comments on Facebook:

"I loved Collin so much. He left his mark on our lives. I believe he was an angel God sent to all of us to teach us how to love. One of my sweet memories was how he loved being in church. I can see him sitting on that back pew, with his legs all stretched out leaning against someone, most of the time Mom. He never wanted to leave. He was a great teacher. I have so many great memories. I feel honored to have been a part of his life."

The same sentiment has been expressed by other friends over the years.

This is a compilation of two posts from Beverly in 2017. October is Down Syndrome awareness month, and our friend Beverly posted:

"I was so blessed at church today when I was invited to visit The Friends of Collin Class. Thank you…for the sweet welcome. If you're not aware of how this class came to be and received its name, then I encourage you to ask! Such a precious story about a precious family! Collin taught us so much. The life of Collin Harris made a difference in mine!"

Our beloved pastor, C.O. Herchenhahn, once said, **"Collin molded and shaped us."**

It has been almost 40 years since we left Stephenville and the Friends of Collin group is still thriving. No doubt, Collin has contributed more to the good of mankind than many of us ever will. The church gave us many opportunities for outings with Collin, including an excursion to Dinosaur Valley Park in Glen Rose, a rocky, watery hike.

Although Collin enjoyed being with friends, eventually he became a little distressed when the footing became difficult, and his clothes got wet. I was at the farm, so a couple of our friends alternated carrying him, resulting in wet clothes for all concerned, but neither friend complained. This was just one of the many times a church friend came to Becky's rescue.

Becky received a phone call from Collin's teacher one morning notifying her that Collin had grown impatient with his task of sorting objects in a jar, slammed the jar against the table, and cut his hand. Becky hurried to school and parked her car. Hoping an emergency room visit could be avoided, Becky calmed Collin in the back seat as his teacher drove them to the house of our friend, a retired pharmacist, who was proficient in first aid. She knew Collin would be comfortable with Milton and allow him to treat the cut without protesting.

After examining his hand, Milton offered to drive them to Fort Worth to a physician who had the equipment and skill to check for and remove any remaining slivers of glass and apply stitches if necessary. Fortunately, the doctor determined there was no remaining glass, and although he preferred stitching the cut, he realized bandaging would be sufficient and less traumatic for Collin. We were so appreciative of our friend Milton, but also of Collin's teacher, who understood the need for assistance in transporting a distressed Collin. He loved the teacher, her assistants, and the music therapist provided in his classroom each week.

Two days a week after school, Becky drove Collin and a classmate to the home of the music therapist for additional therapy. When the success of the music therapist in engaging her students with music came to the attention of the local newspaper, an article was published in the April 7, 1982 edition of Stephenville Empire-Tribune. The following is an excerpt from the article:

"At their first meeting, Collin ignored Cathy. Not the slightest smile creased his face at her antics. The musical games she and the children played held no interest for him. He only sat, shoulders bent, with no response. That was seven months ago. At his private lesson last week Collin, a ten-year-old Down Syndrome child, eagerly picked up the xylophone as Cathy had asked him to. He angled his face to the instrument and concentrated on striking both the large and small keys, not an easy task for him……and as Cathy played and sang, he laughed, because now he can make music, too."

Observing the joy Collin displayed while strumming the guitar with Cathy, I discovered the perfect Christmas present for him. I knew he would be excited. Soon after we were at Becky's folks for celebration of Christmas. As Christmas gifts were being exchanged it came Collin's turn. When he saw the guitar, he grabbed it by the neck and threw it across the room with all his might!! He was definitely EXCITED, but not as I expected. Collin was enraged at the audacity to give him a guitar. Although he couldn't speak, he was very clear in his message. "I ONLY DO THE GUITAR WITH CATHY! HOW DARE YOU TRY TO CUT IN ON THAT!!! This was the first major display of serious obsessive issues. We didn't realize the extent of what might be brewing in years to come.

There were many compassionate people in the community who organized or assisted with Special Olympic events including a race in which Collin was to participate. When the race started, Collin walked slowly behind the others until someone shouted, "Run, Collin! Run!" Collin picked up the pace, crossed the finish line, and continued to run until someone chased after him and took him back to rejoin the other participants.

In unity, the crowd and other participants clapped and cheered as he was escorted back to the starting line. The sportsmanship of the other runners and the crowd's reaction was both typical of these events and inspirational. It was not unusual at these events for one of the participants to turn back and offer encouragement and assistance when someone stumbled during the race.

Although he liked to run and play chase with his cousins, Collin had no understanding of the concept of a race, nor did he experience peer pressure during recess on a hot afternoon. Instead of playing ball with his classmates, Collin sat contently with his teachers under the shade of a large oak tree. He was quite capable of throwing a ball to someone, but if he was handed a ball, he would often look directly at the person, and throw the ball in the opposite direction, laughing at the surprised reaction. Friends and neighbors tolerated his shenanigans, creative and patient as they sought new ways to connect with him. The reaction of strangers was unpredictable.

Our next-door neighbors, Gerre, Jo, and their kids, Julie and Matt, were priceless. The kids were about the same age as ours and our families were very close. The children could be in our house or theirs at about any time. Matt was quite capable of walking in without a knock whenever he wanted. That was fine with us. The first time Gerre came over for a neighborly visit, he sat down and propped his foot on the kitchen table. I knew then that this was going to work. The four adults decided to start walking together in the evening. On the first trip, Jo was ready to go in her house shoes. The walks didn't work out, but the friendship flourished. Julie said, "Collin taught me so very much about loving people with special needs."

Becky's sister, Melanie, and her husband Steve came to visit us one weekend. Melanie recalls a rude awakening in the middle of the night:

"Becky explained that we needed to lock the door or Collin might escape from his room and join us. We were asleep when the door burst open and Collin ran in hollering at the top of his lungs and jumped right in the bed with us. Scared us at first, but it was so comical, we had to laugh. Becky was horrified and apologetic, but it was typical of Collin. I think he understood that we needed some excitement and was happy to provide it!"

Steve remembered the incident, and said that he had some very fond memories of Collin:

"I would have to say that his joining us in bed would have to be my favorite. I loved how Collin could enjoy using a sheet and just being totally covered; sometimes I wish I could get away from things too. I also enjoyed trying my best to communicate with him through sounds. He made unique popping sounds with his mouth and I would try and mimic those sounds in a way to interact and hopefully make him smile. Some of my fondest memories were watching the interaction between Collin and his sisters. Deanne and Amy had a special bond with him and their communications were on a higher level than most of us can even understand. I could see how much they truly loved him and how protective of him they were. I believe Collin made us all a 'little better' in some ways and he was truly a blessing from God!"

Moving to Stephenville and continuing our small farming and cattle operations over 200 miles away was not a practical business decision, but circumstances pretty much required that arrangement. I managed to be in the wrong place much of the time, except during summer months when school was out and we were all at the farm. However, Becky understood the situation and fully supported our joint decision to move to Stephenville. As we expected, it was a bad move financially, yet the move proved to be a financial lifesaver. HUH?

OK, I will tell you why. Please be patient, the explanation will be a little lengthy. We were young and I was foolish. Being young and healthy, "we didn't need no Insurance." When Collin was born, Becky and I had no health coverage that would automatically add a child to the policy at birth, and Collin was uninsurable. After all the children were born, we decided to obtain family health insurance just in case the need arose later. No insurance company we could find would include Collin on an underwritten policy.

Within a couple of years after we moved to Stephenville, Collin was having health issues. He was losing weight and having other problems, but doctors were having difficulty identifying the underlying cause. During that time our daughter Deanne was taking art lessons. One day when Becky picked Deanne up after her art lesson, the art teacher, Kay, expressed concern regarding Collin's declining health and asked Becky if we had health insurance. The art teacher's husband was an insurance agent, and she suggested that he had a policy that could possibly insure the entire family. We were skeptical but spoke with her husband.

Kay's husband explained that a major farm-related organization was changing their group plan to a new insurance carrier. During the transition, members of the organization could obtain health insurance with no medical questions. but only if there was active membership in the farm organization. I faintly remembered being offered a lifetime membership for $25 a few years before, but I couldn't remember with certainty that I had bothered to join.

Quickly checking, we confirmed our membership in the organization, ensuring we could have quality health insurance coverage. What a relief! It had been a "tiny bit" stressful having a sick family member with no insurance. We were fearful that Collin was headed for serious health problems but didn't know what to expect.

Within about 6 months after obtaining health coverage, at twelve years of age, Collin went into heart failure and was rushed to Forth Worth Children's Hospital. Slightly less than five feet tall and weighing 48 pounds, Collin was in dangerous territory. Doctors determined that a tremendously overactive thyroid was the cause of Collin's heart failure. Being too weak for surgery, radioactive iodine treatment was administered. After two weeks of hospitalization following the treatment, he was on a fast pace to recovery and was released from the hospital.

We learned that ICU rules may sometimes be bent if you're respectful. When visiting hours were over the first night in ICU, we stayed long enough that nurses realized we could be helpful and delivered a cot. Our church youth director showed up well past visiting hours in the early morning hours. Dressed in a suit and tie, Jim walked in as though he owned the place, unhindered by the hospital staff. That wasn't his first visit to an ICU after hours to tend his sheep. Jim theorized that no one ever asked who he was for fear of offending a physician.

Approximately two years later, Collin had back-to-back surgeries that left him hospitalized for five continuous weeks. He was admitted for treatment of an ulcerated esophagus and a fundoplication surgery procedure to repair a hiatal hernia. Children with Down Syndrome often have atlantoaxial instability which is sometimes problematic when an airway is inserted during surgery. As luck would have it, vertebrae in his neck slipped which required stabilization to protect the neck of a fourteen-year-old toddler who would not be careful. After sufficient time to recover from the first surgery, a piece of bone was removed from his pelvis to graft to C1-C2 vertebrae for stabilization. Collin recovered nicely and flourished for the next several years.

Answer to how bad financial move was a financial lifesaver: If we had not moved to Stephenville in that time frame, and if Deanne had not taken art lessons from Kay, we would not have had health insurance to cover 7 weeks of very expensive medical services. Think about those probabilities. That was huge to us financially. Seven weeks of hospital charges including heart failure, radioactive iodine treatment, plus two surgeries, one involving the spine, would have been an enormous cost. To have escaped that land mine was nothing short of a miracle.

During his hospital stay, Becky, her mom, and I alternated shifts staying with Collin. Amy and Deanne visited on weekends and attended school on weekdays seventy miles away in Stephenville. Once again, friends and neighbors came to our aid. The girls spent weeknights with Jo and Gerre, walking to our house next door to do laundry and homework. Occasionally Amy stayed with her friend Julie, Beverly's daughter. Deanne and Amy understood the necessity of our absence to care for Collin, and never complained about the situation despite the difficulties. Over the years, the resilience learned at an early age has enabled them to meet challenges and adversity in their adult lives.

While hospitalized, Collin frequently serenaded the entire wing with his bell carousel. Checking with the nurses, we were assured the bells were not causing problems. Collin loved to spin the colorful bells and lightly touch them with a stick, pen, or other object to produce a soft, melodious sound as the bells spun around. Watching the bells spin and hearing the soothing tones occupied him for hours. I can still see Collin yanking strings of balloons as the air vent sent the balloons in rotation above his bed. When a string got within reach, Collin would yank it, watch it drift off, realign, and drift back over for another yank. It was a hit when Grandma tied a balloon to his toe. His hospital room was an active one. Not many have balloons rotating around the bed with bells ringing.

During these five weeks of surgeries and continuous hospitalization, Becky and I became acquainted with about everyone on that wing of Fort Worth Children's Hospital. Melissa, a patient across the hall, was having treatments for a few days and her parents couldn't be with her. She didn't say much. Her legs and arms were too small and weak for much use. She couldn't walk or turn over in the bed, confined to wherever she was placed. Melissa spent some time in a wheelchair at the nurse's station, and the nurses allowed me to roll her around the halls. I introduced her to Collin, but he just ignored her. That was it.

A couple of days later, the parents came to take Melissa home. I introduced myself and leaned over the bed to say something to Melissa. She stared at me intently for a bit, and then said, "I love you." As my cheeks began to get wet, I replied, "I love you too." Then she said, "I pray for your little boy." I don't remember what I said as my collar got wet, but I have thought of Melissa and repeated her story many times. Can you imagine being in Melissa's condition, but still having such a pure heart to be concerned about somebody else? Melissa touched me and indirectly many others.

During those weeks, I spent some time in the pediatric intensive care waiting room. You can see worry in a parent's eyes. I sometimes asked someone if they had a family member in ICU. Quite often parents welcomed the opportunity to share with a complete stranger their experiences and worries for a child threatened by illness or injury. No one was ever offended by my asking.

One evening, one of the nurses who had been particularly attentive stopped by after his shift ended. After exchanging pleasantries, he politely asked if we would mind answering a few questions. How were we able to deal with the stress and complexities of caring for Collin? He remarked that we appeared composed and cheerful despite the obvious challenges. What enabled us to remain hopeful as we faced an uncertain future for a child whom we so obviously cherished?

The nurse had witnessed a bevy of family and friends visiting Collin during his hospital stay. We shared with him how their love and support, our belief in the promise of Romans 8:28, and previously answered prayers gave us comfort and hope for the future. We learned early on the value of taking life one day at a time and pulling together. Some days we faced difficulties, other days we witnessed miracles. With tears in his eyes, he thanked us for sharing our story.

Living in Stephenville was one of the greatest experiences of our life for many reasons. We made some of our dearest lifelong friends during the time we lived there. From the strong church to great neighbors and friends, to obtaining health insurance just in the nick of time, we could not have been more blessed. I was away from home a lot, yet Becky and I were comfortable in the knowledge that in my absence, there was always backup five minutes away, 24/7.

It was a time filled with wonderful memories and a few funny incidents that were awkward at the time, but now amusing remembrances. Becky loved going to the library at Tarleton State University. Collin wasn't the most patient cohort. If he became bored, he would find a way to change the plan. As Becky was going through the card catalog (that's what they had in those days), Collin got restless and was ready to leave. As she tells it, she saw Collin reach his arm straight out to the side.

At about the same time an athletic handsome young man walked by. WHACK! Collin had popped the guy on the backside as he walked by. No big deal except for the instant reaction from the young man. For a moment he thought Becky was the perpetrator and was stunned. As she turned beet red and mumbled an apology, he realized Collin was the guilty culprit. He walked away and burst out laughing. Becky took Collin and went home as was his plan.

As previously mentioned, we had moved to Stephenville because of the strong Special Needs program in the public school system. There was no disappointment. The staff became close friends. Collin loved the program and did well. His class was in a temporary building away from the main building. One of the teachers took Collin with her for a meeting, unrelated to him, at the principal's office. Suddenly they missed him!

He was nowhere to be found near the office. The front door and an adjacent busy street were within only yards of the office. Panic was setting in when he was found. Collin had simply gone back to his room. To get there required going outside and navigating past a couple of other buildings. It surprised everyone Collin knew the way.

One summer Becky and the kids spent several days in South Texas with family, including with a special outing to South Padre Island. While all the kids waded along the shore and fed the seagulls, Collin sat at the water's edge, squealing in delight at the soaring birds and gentle waves washing over his legs as sand flowed in and out of his clothes. Collin was drenched in salt water with a considerable amount of sand in his shorts causing discomfort, but he was reluctant to leave the beach, and there was no private shower to remedy the situation. Becky's brother-in-law, Steve, volunteered to help her shower him in the men's restroom while other family members stood guard at the door.

Unfortunately, Collin did not understand the concept that "all good things must end." When the time came for the long trek home after the trip to the beach, Collin balked at the prospect of getting in the car. Sensing her dilemma, his cousin Gilbert approached, ready to intervene if needed. Collin surmised Gilbert could rescue him from her clutches. He grabbed a belt loop on Gilbert's jeans, and looked at Becky defiantly, as if to say, "Whatcha gonna do now, Mama?" Gilbert playfully and gently picked him up and carried him to the car.

There were a couple of lakes within about 30 miles of our house that we frequented. The kids all loved boat rides. We unloaded the boat at Lake Granbury and pitched a tent. Everyone decided to go in the tent for a while before loading up in the boat. NO WAY! Collin was NOT going in that tent.

The tent in our backyard was one thing, (he loved it), but the lake was a different story. He sensed the possibility of getting left in the tent while the boat was in use. What did we do? The choices were to get in the boat or post someone outside the tent with Collin. We loaded everybody up in the boat sooner than planned and hit the lake.

One of my favorite fishing stories is about another Lake Granbury trip. During the spring the sand bass were super easy to catch. They would strike at anything that hit the water. We took the three kids and assisted the girls with their rods and reels and attached a cork to a string for Collin to toss into the water. Deanne and Amy would cast out, reel in, and occasionally catch a fish. Collin would throw his cork out, pull it in, and repeat the motion. The kids were having a blast. Of course, I wanted to enhance Collin's experience.

I tied a small fish on the end of his string just past the cork and threw it out for him. That did not work at all for him, and his fishing experience was OVER! As soon as he felt the weight of the fish he was done and refused to toss the cork again. In fact, he was done with the entire excursion. Why did I try to improve on perfection? I reasoned that it was time to end the casting anyway. At least, that was my story and I stuck to it.

Collin had a low tolerance for any alteration once a plan was in motion. Our friend Beverly frequently stopped by our house. One day as she was leaving, she off-handedly remarked, "Come go home with me Collin," a comment not meant to be taken seriously. To Collin, her words were a literal invitation. He was excited and ready to go!

Surprised, Beverly asked, "What do I do now?" Becky said, "Sorry, but he is taking you up on your offer. I'll follow and bring him back." Nothing less was going to work. Upon arrival at Beverly's house, Collin ran gleefully into the living room and immediately removed his shoes. After Becky and Beverly enjoyed coffee and a short visit, Becky persuaded Collin to put his shoes back on and go home with her. The use of his shoes was frequently a means to express himself.

Incidentally, while in Stephenville, Collin grasped the concept of money (pretty good for his mental age) and learned to use a straw. Collin loved French fries, and learned that if he saw the big yellow "M," a trip to the drive-through meant he could present a coupon (a yellow strip of paper) at the window and be rewarded with French fries. One day we picked up his fries at the window, then changed plans and went inside to order drinks and burgers.

At first, he decided sitting under the table would be more fun, but we coaxed him out of his hiding place and offered him a Coke. Straws had always been a mystery to him, but as one of the girls used the straw to drop sips in his mouth, he suddenly began to suck on the straw. When they placed the other end back in the cup, he was elated to realize that he could use the straw without help. Our applause and cheers caused a few funny reactions from the other diners, but we couldn't contain our excitement! NOT ONLY had Collin displayed his rudimentary concept of money in the form of a McDonald's coupon, but he had learned how to use a straw!!!

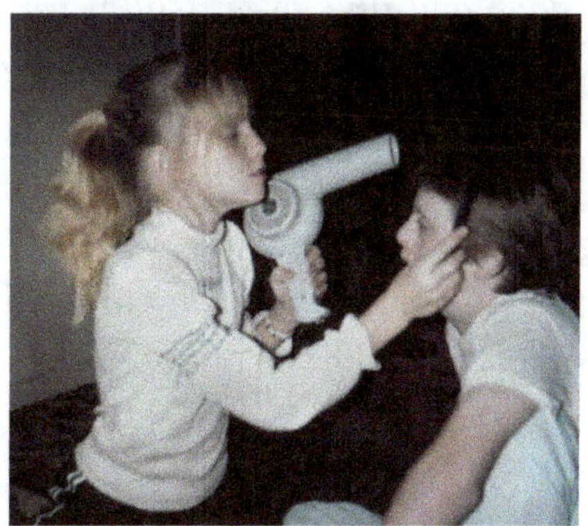

CHAPTER FIVE
INTERIM MOVE

After six years in Stephenville, circumstances required we briefly move closer to the farm. We moved to Floydada, which by then had a program that worked for Collin. He was 15 years old and doing well. We missed our friends in Stephenville but made new ones when we joined the First Baptist Church in Floydada. Though it was a brief stay, Collin made friends and cast some pebbles. Wherever we lived, friends found new ways to form connections with Collin. Some of our favorite memories from that time were related to an obsession of Collin's. He had discovered the sensation of wearing a scarf or sheet over his head and feeling the wind blowing through it.

Amy's classmate and friend Jennifer commented,

"When you guys first moved next door, we were slightly shocked to open our front door and find sweet Collin perched on our front porch! He had his sheet and was enjoying watching it flapping in the wind. Soon it became a common occurrence, and we loved watching him with his sheet or scarf. He was in his happy place. He was a sweet soul, and his laugh is not forgotten! He was precious!" If a breeze whisked his scarf away, Jennifer was happy to provide a replacement. Jennifer's mom said, "*Collin was a special blessing and sweet memory. Loved him!*".

For a long while, Collin was more likely to be seen with a scarf covering his head than not. Our friend Dennis seized on this opportunity. One weekend he and his family joined us on a bowling outing about 20 miles away in Plainview. While driving through the city, Dennis draped a scarf over his head and cap, generating surprised looks from a few fellow motorists. That was Dennis' plan. Collin always responded positively to our friends' attempts to form these strange connections. Amy described Collin's bowling as "*the lazy way.... sit down and roll the ball. Easy way.... just run down the lane, no ball needed.*"

I suppose it's a character flaw in me, but one of my favorite Collin stories took place in Floydada. Collin had a great ear for music and loved it, especially the good stuff. Offer him a choice of Streisand or country music, which I love, he would take Streisand every time. Nothing wrong with that, but he began to require a certain level of talent for someone performing in public. We had arrived at Church late and had to sit near the front of the church, in the middle section of the pew.

A lady was having difficulty with a particular song and hit a succession of off-key notes. Collin began snorting with each missed note and was getting louder with each outburst, to the point of yelling. I had no choice but to pick him up, maneuver to the middle aisle, and take him outside. Collin was livid! He wanted to strongly display his disgust but had no intention of leaving. He was hitting me about the head and shoulders as we made our exit. Our friend Dennis witnessed that situation; there aren't adjectives to describe it. Listening to Dennis tell the story, was almost as funny as the incident.

In Floydada there were picnics, Special Olympics events, and church socials. Once again, Collin was warmly welcomed by the neighbors, his teachers, and others in the community. Collin never learned to swim. but he loved splashing in the shallow end of the pool with the other children. A couple of the dads joined the kids in the pool and kept a watchful eye, ready to rescue Collin if he ventured too close to the deep end. We only lived in Floydada a little over a year. When we moved away, his teacher and friends sent photos, drawings, and letters.

CHAPTER SIX
OMINOUS WARNINGS

The next stop was Abilene in January of 1988. Collin was almost 17. The school system had a good special needs program. Becky opened a bakery, and I eventually began selling insurance. One of the reasons for becoming an insurance agent was that as a captive agent, I was able to procure excellent health insurance for our family without underwriting. The group plan that saved our neck in Stephenville saved many necks. "Everybody" that was sick and could get on the group plan without underwriting enrolled, and claims were enormous. Necessary rate increases eliminated almost everyone, including us, in that specific group within a very short time.

My office was close to home, and Becky had reliable help at the bakery. Flexibility was imperative for both of us because Collin's behavior was becoming less and less predictable and we never knew when either or both of our schedules would be suddenly altered. Amy and Deanne were in high school. They were troopers and always ready to help in any way needed, whether staying with Collin at home or working in the bakery.

Often at the end of the day, we all gathered at home for dinner and then went to the bakery to prepare for the following morning. Becky and the girls decorated birthday cakes, made bread dough, and checked orders and inventory. I had never been much of a cook, but I occasionally rolled out dough. The girls found it quite amusing when I requested the purchase of a larger rolling pin. At times, I helped

Becky finish up pastries and cleaning, but I was primarily the quality control guy. It took a lot of "sampling" to make certain everything was done exactly right. I still carry some of those samples around.

Late one night the girls had been out front cleaning as country music played on Collin's boom box. As they took Collin by the hand and started dancing and twirling, a police cruiser drove slowly by the glass storefront, checking out what must have seemed a strange sight at that hour of the night. Dancing in the bakery, or dancing at home was a common occurrence.

Amy started keeping the books at the bakery when she was 15 and loved it. That may have propelled her into her current accounting profession. The girls were not overly sensitive about Collin but were fiercely defensive of him. The joke was that somebody might do something to Collin and get away with it with us as parents, but **NOT THE GIRLS. DON'T EVEN THINK ABOUT IT!! AND THAT WAS NO JOKE.** By the way, they can relate Collin jokes and stories with the best of them. Our girls had some unique experiences. Deanne had a date with a young man wearing a Western hat. Everybody in Texas knows you don't mess with a guy's hat. Not only did Collin mess with the guy's hat, he also decided to chaperone and ran out the door to accompany them on the date. I don't remember exactly what transpired, but Collin did not chaperone, and the guy came back. Apparently, not too much damage was done.

Amy also had to deal with Collin's reaction to a boyfriend. He became upset that she was sitting next to this guy on the couch. If this had been a movie script, Collin's rendition of the script was a few degrees off. He ran up and hit Amy. This fellow had been around the house before. He and Collin were familiar with each other and had interacted positively on previous occasions. Why he reacted as he did at that moment is only a guess, but Amy thinks he was jealous that she was spending time with the guy rather than him.

Though embarrassed, Amy was not upset at Collin. She just reassured him and spoke soothingly until he became calm. This guy also came back. Amy recalls these incidents as Collin's attempts to be "protective in his own special way. Some boys did not pass the test when we were teenagers."

The girls' friends accepted and interacted with Collin. I'm sure they were surprised when they saw socks hanging from the ceiling fan, one of Collin's favorite targets when his socks came off, or if they watched him pour water in his ear from a glass. He even went cruising with them on occasion. They were unfazed by the unpredictability of what might transpire on these excursions as they met other teens at the local hangouts.

Undeterred, two of their friends eventually worked with others with special needs. One of their friends shared, "Collin was the first person I met with Down Syndrome. I am thankful every day for the opportunity to help others have a voice." Unfazed by Collin's bizarre behavior, another young woman who spent quite a bit of time with Collin became a nurse and worked at Abilene State School.

Collin's intolerance for less-than-stellar performances of music continued throughout his life. We visited a church in Abilene where the youth choir, including a few of Deanne and Amy's friends, were singing. Remember the incident in Floydada when I carried Collin out of church because he didn't like the singing? Yep, he did it again in Abilene. Unfortunately, he was bigger and stronger and it required Mom's help this time.

I grabbed him under his shoulders, and Becky grabbed his feet. We hastily exited the church door, which unfortunately opened close to the street. Imagine the surprise of the passersby! Deanne and Amy stayed for the rest of the service, and their friends attempted to finish the performance without bursting into laughter!

One afternoon Deanne and Collin were in a department store standing in line at the cash register. Standing in line wasn't Collin's thing. When he began to kick the counter and knock clothes off the rack, Deanne was quickly invited to move to the front of the line and check out. She offered thanks to the other customers, said "he doesn't get out much," paid the cashier, and they went home. And… Collin did not have to wait in line.

One of Deanne's most hilarious experiences with Collin happened when she got out of her car at the grocery store to pick up a flyer from the outside rack. Collin never set foot out of the car if he was barefooted. But never say never. Barefooted, Collin got out of the car and stepped in bubble gum. Of course, he didn't like it. By the time they got back home, bubble gum reached from feet to hair, to clothes, and parts unknown.

I bet you can't hold an almost empty glass of water, extend your arm up as high as you can, turn your head sideways, and pour the remaining water from the glass into your ear. I'm not talking about pouring the water near the ear. IN THE EAR. DEAD CENTER. EVERY TIME. Collin could do that. Nobody would have thought of even the possibility of teaching him this trick. Why would they? Why he decided to attempt and then perfect this feat is yet another question. That might be a good game for adults to play when the kids aren't watching. Whoever can fill their ear full of water from a glass a foot above their head, without getting their clothes wet, wins the prize. What should the prize be?

He also enjoyed pulling a toboggan over his face and running blindly through the house, bumping into whatever lay in his path. The more attention he received the more he enjoyed it. NOTHING brought more cheer to Collin than the sound of dropped silverware or shattering glass, which was always followed by Collin's laughter. Fortunately, he didn't decide to purposely create those sounds himself. You can't imagine how grateful we were that he didn't think of that. Although he was only a few pounds lighter than his sisters, he thought it appropriate to be picked up and carried around the house for his entertainment. Why not? It was fun.

I taught Collin a few things that maybe should have first been cleared through Becky. She may still be a "little" aggravated. Collin knew the sign for more, touching the ends of his fingers together. He sometimes used that sign at the table. The sign was usually displayed under the table, out of sight, yet everyone was expected to see it.

Don't ask me why because there is no decent explanation. I encouraged Collin to stomp his foot and bang the table with his plastic glass when he wanted more to drink, and nobody responded to his unseen sign. He soon skipped the sign and went straight for the gusto, stomping his foot and banging the table. Collin was highly amused. Mama "was not" amused. We have dents in our dining table. We should have replaced the table years ago, but those are Collin's dents.

Luckily, I didn't get divorced. That's fortunate because Becky and I would have had a big fight over who had to take Collin; neither of us would have claimed him as kin. He couldn't have been ours! My goodness, this is the guy who emptied his water glass by pouring it in his ear, made certain his socks were rotating on the ceiling fan, obstructed his vision by design to blindly crash through the house, and dented the tabletop when he wanted more! OOPS! I taught him that one.

Collin did funny things, entertained himself and those around him, and brought much joy to our home. We didn't recognize that some of his demands and reactions were also ominous signs of what might come. Collin was showing increased signs of obsessive behavior, often agitated by the smallest deviation or interruption from routine.

We could not have fathomed the problems looming on the horizon. We knew his behaviors were becoming problematic but thought we could deal with it. Collin was eventually informally diagnosed with being on the autism spectrum. That, combined with maturing, lower-end IQ, and other unknown issues, created an explosive combination.

Public school systems provide special transportation for special needs children. The bus Collin rode initially had a monitor with whom he readily connected. He loved the monitor and loved to ride the bus. It was a reward twice a day to ride that bus. After some time, a new person was assigned as the monitor. The new monitor and Collin did not positively connect. That was likely because of Collin's unacceptance of any replacement for the previous monitor, whom he considered a friend, and whose company he enjoyed.

Collin didn't like the monitor and his reaction was inappropriate. He went out of his way to antagonize her. He refused to sit down or comply with any directions. She reported the behavior, and we were informed Collin could no longer ride the bus. The repercussion was not unexpected.

We understood the dilemma. We took Collin to and from school for a couple of days before the school contacted us again to assure us that "someone" would transport Collin the following day. Imagine Becky's surprise the next morning when the aforementioned "someone" pulled into our driveway in a limo! She learned that the driver had been given no information regarding his passenger. Becky was relieved that the driver was unfazed by the situation and that Collin was quite content when the friendly chauffeur escorted him into the back seat.

After school, the limo returned, and the chauffeur reported that Collin was "a perfect little gentleman." Collin loved the arrangement! Amy describes the situation as "my favorite example of a highly successful peaceful protest against social injustice." The limo rides were a short-term fix, and arrangements were soon made that worked for Collin on another bus. Very few students have chauffeured limousine transportation to their school, even for a few days.

During this time frame, when Collin was about 20 years of age, he began bruising himself in various ways, banging his knee on the school desk or elbowing himself on his side. Then he started with fists to the face. The danger signals missed were rapidly escalating. Late to mature, issues seemed to compound as the hormones kicked in. Collin lost all ability to tolerate frustration of any kind. His frustrations were not as one might think. He didn't have the mental capacity to have all the normal urges of maturing. As the self-injury episodes began, those frustrations and triggers became mostly unknown and unpredictable. They could seriously present without warning.

What do you do? We started with prescribed Xanax. It barely helped if at all. Before we had any idea of the scope of the problem, Collin was looking for opportunities to hit himself with a fist, or being very limber, strike himself with a knee to the face or forehead. The escalation occurred rapidly over the span of one day. Following a particularly vicious episode we took him to the emergency room at a local hospital. All they could do was check him for concussion, restrain him, and administer a strong sedative.

Luckily, there was a State School facility with an infirmary in Abilene. Collin was admitted to the infirmary on a temporary emergency basis. Their recommendation was to enroll him in State School, but institutionalizing him was inconceivable to us. He was restrained in bed for most of his temporary stay. After a couple of weeks back at home the episodes escalated again.

Going much beyond what was required, Abilene Regional MHMR (Mental Health Mental Retardation) Center and Abilene State School systems worked together to provide State School services on an outpatient basis. At that time, this was the first and only experiment of this nature in Abilene. One-on-one supervision and personalized therapy were provided for two years at Abilene State School. His progress was monitored and recorded, creating a useful tool in programs across Texas to train caregivers dealing with self-injurious behaviors.

We took Collin to State school each morning and picked him up in the afternoon. At home, he was closely monitored during the day. During the night one of us often stayed with him in case he awakened and became upset. Becky and I alternated shifts, but occasionally the girls took turns. I joked with them not to tell their friends at school that they were sleeping with their 21-year-old brother. They "got it" and eventually confirmed that they had immediately shared my comment with their friends.

The State School program ended after 2 years. On the recommendation of MHMR, we placed Collin in a group home. He had made some progress but still needed almost constant observation. As always, we made daily contact, usually multiple times, and Collin seemed to be mostly content. Some professionals suggest a workshop setting and regular schedule is beneficial to a mentally challenged individual, and that is the case for many individuals. However, on the days Collin was sent to the workshop, he was usually more agitated.

Eventually, they discontinued the workshop trips, and Collin was more content for a while. One of the caregivers from the group home would occasionally take Collin for a ride in his convertible after his shift. Collin loved the wind blowing his hair back as they rode to the bakery for a treat or just went cruising.

After about a year in the group home, he went off the rails and required being strapped to a gurney to transport him to State School for enrollment. That was a bad day. It is difficult to imagine and impossible to describe the horror of realizing that left alone unrestrained for a few hours, your son would most likely destroy himself, and we didn't know how to help him. HOWEVER, buoyed by Romans 8:28 and generations of "pulling together," we were hopeful and confident in the future.

It was during this time that Becky's bakery orders and catering events increased significantly. As word spread about an upcoming particularly busy weekend, Becky's sisters and my brother Gene came to town to help out in the bakery. Melanie visited Collin in the infirmary, carefully sewing name labels on his clothes before joining Jessica and Judy as they filled and delivered orders. Although they still joke about being a little overwhelmed, they pitched in and got the job done. At the time it was imperative that I be with Collin, so Gene offered to help Becky deliver a huge very heavy wedding cake adorned with gum paste grapes. As Becky and Gene struggled to unload the cake and enter the front door of the Abilene Country Club, to her dismay, Becky noticed a grape slowly rolling to the edge of a tier. After carefully placing the cake on the table, Becky asked Gene about the errant grape. His response: "I ate it!"

Once again, Collin was initially protected by restraints in bed in the infirmary. He was also given some meds to help take some of the edge off. The drugs may have helped a little, but nothing was found to have a significant effect. It became obvious after several days of restraint that Collin had to come out of that bed. The problem was that there were safety protocols that kept State School from risking injury by releasing him from the restraints. Fortunately, those protocols didn't apply to parents. With the approval of the State School staff, Becky and I released him and walked him over campus, one of us on either side.

Walking Collin over campus was no stroll in the park. We dragged him upright, with him taking hesitant steps, over the campus. That was very trying in every aspect. There were many head butts to get us off him while trying to drop down to bang his head on the ground. Awful as it was, this was an almost daily routine for weeks. Nobody knew if this effort would be of any benefit, but we continued the walks. Sometimes he would touch us gently during the episodes, as if to say, "It's OK." After a time, Collin's resistance subsided somewhat, and we could have a walk that all of us enjoyed.

Collin could be bribed sometimes. He loved Cokes, knew it took quarters at the machine, and recognized the Coke button to push. Though he was still restrained while in bed, we tempted him to allow us to release him from restraints. When we offered quarters to him, he knew we were offering to take him to the Coke machine for a treat. If he took the quarters, we could walk him down the hall to the Coke machine without incident. He would insert the quarters, push the Coke button, and get his Coke. If he would not take the quarters, we wouldn't dare release him.

Over several weeks, self-injurious behavior (SIB) subsided considerably, although we can't be certain why. The infirmary was generally quiet. Collin was in the infirmary for three months before being assigned to a dorm. Although he continued to have some episodes of SIB, based on his health and behavior he could have been moved earlier, but it took some time for staff to find the most appropriate dorm to best fit his needs.

We loved the State School System in Abilene. They did the best they could for every single individual on campus and did a great job. Fortunately, Becky and I had no restraints on the time we spent on campus. One or both of us were almost always with Collin during the day, but leaving before bedtime. First and equal priorities, we didn't interfere with caregivers and respected the other residents in every way. After that, we were available to assist Collin if needed, take him for walks, and occasionally assisted other residents at mealtime, with approval of supervisor when the dorm was short-staffed.

Deanne and Amy made regular visits to see Collin when he was in the infirmary. We advised them that the dorm experience would be quite different and that it might be best if we brought Collin outside for their visits. Occasionally the girls accompanied us on walks but also visited the dorm.

One day while Amy was sitting with Collin, one of the residents who was considered a fall risk unexpectedly jumped from his chair and barreled out the door. With no thought of her own safety, Amy ran to catch him. Fortunately, one of the staff noticed, immediately followed and persuaded the resident to return with him to the dorm. Deanne and Amy were comfortable in the dorm, kind to the residents and always greeted them with smiles and acceptance.

The time we spent within the confines of the State School campus had a profound effect on us. Want a greater understanding of basic human nature? Spend time observing adult-age toddlers who do not have the mental capacity to conceal emotions or lie. Want to have a greater appreciation for your fellow man? Observe the selfless efforts of State School personnel without nearly enough pay and sometimes not enough respect.

I suppose in some circumstances, the most difficult element in diagnosing and deciding on proper treatment for the mentally-challenged often stems from a lack of ways to communicate. Collin was non-verbal. Although he understood much, he could not discuss anything with anyone. We couldn't ask him where it hurt or what was bothering him and expect an answer, even if he understood and had an answer. He was immensely frustrated at times and could not help us help him.

Along those lines, I remember asking one of the mental health professionals if he thought Collin had a chemical imbalance. His answer was an EMPHATIC YES but added that the problem is identifying which of the hundreds of chemicals is out of balance. He told me of a young lady with nearly the same level of self-injurious behavior (SIB) as Collin. After many unsuccessful outcomes with other medications, Prozac was prescribed. IT WORKED PERFECTLY!! Hoping they had found the "magic bullet," they tried Prozac on dozens of other individuals with zero effect. Unfortunately, the story continued.

The young lady was on a strong dosage of Prozac, and staff felt it necessary to gradually reduce the dosage level if possible. After a few incremental reductions, the self-injury returned and was never again brought under control, even after increasing the Prozac dosage. Sometimes the only thing that can be done is all you can do to treat symptoms without completely understanding the basic problem or long-term effects of any treatment path. That is tough stuff. I have the greatest respect for those who must make life-altering decisions every day without all the information they need. The pressure they are under is enormous.

When self-injurious behavior is presented, what do you do?

A question we all asked ourselves was "Is restraint always the best move? Could it be, if the behavior is ignored, he might injure himself less, then stop without the fight?" Maybe. That was tried at times. Generally, Collin would show you just how much more dangerous the situation could be if his behavior was ignored.

Every situation was different, and no one was ever totally confident in what action or non-action should be implemented.

Temporary restraint until he calmed down was the general protocol. Collin had many weapons. If you blocked a punch from one hand the other fist was on its way. Block both fists, his knee might immediately strike his forehead with great force, blacking both eyes. He could have been a martial arts expert. Quick as a cat, he always knew the openings to get in a lick. His fists and knees were his most utilized weapons, but there were others including door frames, that he could bang against.

Restraining Collin was often a battle. He was under five feet tall, weighed less than 100 pounds, but was much stronger than he appeared. The “basket hold”, holding the person from behind by the wrists with his arms crossed in front of him, is often an effective technique to control someone to prevent injury. However, proximity of the restrainer’s head to Collin’s head required some care. Quite often, Collin attempted headbutting to get free from his captor. It was important to not allow distance between heads. Distance allowed a harder whack. If Collin’s head pulled away, we followed with our head to minimize the head butt.

To protect his head and eyes during SIB episodes State School tried a helmet. He hit the helmet with his fists until his hands were so damaged, he couldn’t close his fist to hold a spoon. After his hands healed, he had to be retrained to feed himself. That wasn’t a quick fix either. Another issue was removing the helmet while he ate, or while bathing him. As he became dependent on the helmet, he would resist removal and was subject to injury. Ultimately, a decision was made to discontinue the helmet. Sometimes, such decisions are made based upon best judgment call of which route is the least dangerous. That is often much like a roll of the dice, but a decision has to be made.

State School protocol required individuals with new bruises to be taken to the clinic as a precaution to assess the extent of the injury, performing x-rays if deemed necessary. Sometimes Collin would return to the dorm with additional bruises. He didn’t intend to do the clinic thing. What do you do?

Collin's destructive behavior, though almost continuous at times, was interrupted by periods of sporadic, though unpredictable, shorter, and/or less intense episodes. One of the mental health staff told me that once self-injurious behavior (SIB) began it was generally very difficult to stop. SIB manifests itself in many ways unique to each individual. He also said those individuals would often find reinforcement to continue SIB, regardless of how you responded.

We observed a man with Down Syndrome about the same age and IQ as Collin, very pleasant but restrained in a wheelchair, recovering from neck surgery. He had broken his neck twice by karate chopping himself. He appeared calm and relaxed as they released him from restraints.

With a big smile, he immediately reached up and karate-chopped his neck. I assume some type of mechanical protection was attempted to prevent damage to his neck from his hands, but that may have been a daunting task. Anyone with a singular goal can be more cunning and inventive than thought possible. Never take the bet that you cannot be outsmarted by someone with an extremely low IQ.

Collin was an exceptionally tough case. It is important to note that not everyone who self-injures is as determined, forceful, or as explosive as Collin. PLEASE DO NOT ASSUME YOUR INTELLECTUALLY DISABLED CHILD IS LIKELY TO BECOME SELF-INJURIOUS. Collin's situation was NOT THE NORM. However, I believe it is prudent to seek professional advice if unusual behaviors occur.

Collin's dorm housed twenty-eight individuals. Some were about the same mental level as Collin. Some were slightly higher level intellectually but with other disabilities. With budget restraints, there was a minimal staff of only five during the day. We had zero complaints concerning the State School system but preferred an environment with a better ratio of staff to residents in a smaller setting. We continued to have a good relationship with the administrators of MHMR and State School, and when we discussed alternate placement for Collin, they produced a huge notebook containing phone numbers, locations, and other pertinent information about group home providers throughout Texas. We spent considerable time on the phone discussing Collin's situation and visited several possibilities.

Some providers were willing to consider placement, but further conversations revealed inexperience in dealing with Collin's type of behavior. Finally, we found a group home organization in San Antonio that seemed like a good prospect. That organization (no longer active in the same capacity) was confident they could meet Collin's needs.

Becky and I were ecstatic but apprehensive at the prospects. First, no one from the group home had observed Collin on site. We were anxious whether Collin would be accepted after further evaluation. Second, even if accepted into the program, there was no guarantee the program could deliver the results for which we hoped.

During the first visit from the group home team, Collin showcased some of his worst behavior. Although we wanted staff to be aware of Collin's worst behaviors, we feared the group home would decline to accept him because of what they saw. Following observation, and with no hesitation, they expressed confidence that they had the skills and resources Collin needed. A second group home visit was scheduled. We didn't know who might view Collin on the second visit and were apprehensive about whether the second team would agree with the initial evaluation.

There were other considerations as well. Moving to San Antonio would require uprooting, moving farther from Deanne and Amy, and starting our businesses over from scratch yet again. What if we made the plunge and nothing worked out as planned? That was a real possibility. How could we predict if the group home results would meet expectations? Could we be diving into a failed venture, leaving Collin in a less desirable situation than where he was?

Those unanswerable questions briefly ran through our minds, but not for long. Regardless of the risks, Becky and I were determined to go for it if given the opportunity. The second visit from group home personnel confirmed Collin's acceptance into their program. After a few weeks of processing, in the summer of 1997, Collin, Becky, and I were headed to San Antonio.

State School stepped in with all their hearts and covered a lot of the risks for Collin's placement. He had been in their facility for approximately nine months and that organization wanted nothing less than the very best results for Collin. They furloughed Collin for thirty days with the assurance that he could return to his familiar environment if the placement was not satisfactory. That was a **VERY VALUABLE PROTECTION,** relieving a lot of our anxiety in attempting to make such a drastic change. Hoping to ensure a smooth transition, Abilene State School had two caregivers transport Collin in a van to the group home in San Antonio.

Although the State School offered to have the two caregivers stay to assist for a couple of days, the group home graciously declined the offer, as they wanted to hit the ground running with their approach. There was one other resident in the home with rotating staff. Additionally, a stout young man was designated to be by Collin's side 16 hours a day for his protection.

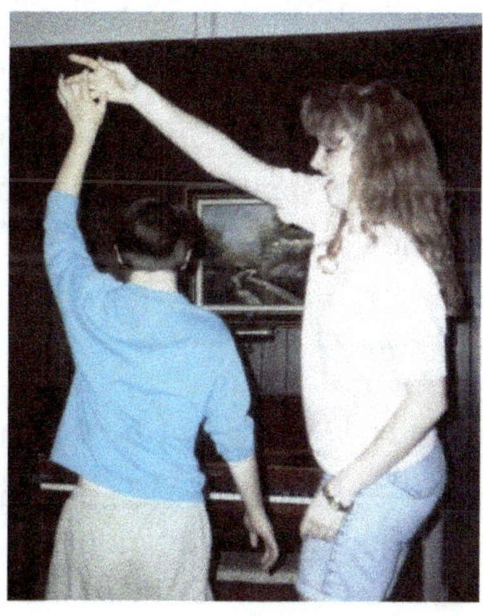

CHAPTER SEVEN
HOPE TO HEARTBREAK

What a wonderful relief! At age 26, Collin was entering into a major new chapter of his life. We were immediately impressed with the staff and plan of care. Despite the challenges, we were confident Collin would have a good shot at the very best possible care 24/7. From the first day, the administration assumed Collin was a permanent resident, never doubting the program would be successful.

I must say that the group home not only SALVAGED Collin but also Becky and me. Though Becky and I were maintaining, by the time they stepped in we were both at our wits end emotionally and mentally as well as physically exhausted. Within a few days, we were comfortable enough with the move to go headlong into it, making San Antonio our permanent home.

The following summer Deanne quit her teaching job in the Fort Worth area and moved to San Antonio, visiting Collin often. Fulfilling her dream since childhood, Amy was working as a CPA in Dallas, making frequent trips to San Antonio. The group home was the scene of many family gatherings including birthdays and other celebrations. On more than one occasion, we transported Thanksgiving turkey and all the trimmings to share with Collin and his caregivers.

Deanne began dating a young man, and within a short time, he accompanied her on her visits to see Collin. Trent always squeezed Collin's shoulders with a gentle shake to make certain Collin would recognize him, always eliciting a smile. Guess who Deanne and Trent first announced their engagement to? Yep, you're right! Oh, how Trent and Collin loved each other. Trent was as a brother to Collin and is more like a son to us than a son-in-law.

That program brought us peace and introduced us to some of the most precious people, whom we deeply appreciated. Collin had "1-on-1" supervision 16 hours per day, so a visit with Collin was also a visit with his caregiver. During those visits, we enjoyed conversations with kind, generous people with various cultural, geographical, and religious differences. We gained new perspectives and mutual respect.

One evening after a long day at work, I stopped by to see Collin. We exchanged high-fives and joked in our customary way. As I sat on the couch next to him, we both dozed off to the soothing sounds of classics on Collin's CD player. When I awoke, Collin was sound asleep with his head in my lap. I had wilted over him and slept with my head on his back as the caregiver sat quietly nearby.

Please let me give a shoutout to two wonderful human beings among many who were integral in Collin's care. Bekah and Richard were a part of the larger group home organization but closely aligned with providing for Collin's individual needs. Bekah was one of Collin's early caregivers, later as a supervisor, who was involved with him throughout his time in the group home. They immediately formed a strong relationship. Regardless of the issues of the day, Bekah could "fix" them when she was on duty.

Bekah told us she could "spill her guts" to Collin, and he wouldn't repeat any of it. I believe, without using words, Collin could spill his guts to her. They were good for each other with a strong loving bond. Bekah is married and has a wonderful family we love as our own. Richard was the director of Collin's program. He had a special-needs daughter and understood the challenges from every aspect: individual, family, and care organization. There was none better in our corner than Richard. Like Bekah, Richard is family to us. Becky and I share a special relationship with them that will endure until the end.

We understood there were dangers at the facility, as in any environment, but we felt and still feel, they gave Collin the best opportunity for some quality of life with protection. They gave him the love and intense services necessary to transform his state of being for the better.

AND…while Collin was being redirected as needed, he did some redirecting himself. Collin loved the sensation of a blow dryer on his hair, wet or dry didn't matter. That was GOOD STUFF. A young lady presented Collin with a proposition. He was assured that after he had completed a certain task, she would reward him with the warm air from the blow dryer. That sounds reasonable. Right? NOT TO COLLIN! From his standpoint, someone was trying to use something that was already FREE as LEVERAGE against him. I'll cut to the chase. He got his hair blown and the task was not mentioned to him again.

It is important to understand that, even during the worst of Collin's struggles, there were periods of levity on his part and all of us around him. That is strange but thankfully true. A funny exchange with a friend centered on our multiple moves related to Collin. He knew me well and was aware of our moves and situation. I was joking with him that my financial adviser was mentally challenged and self-injurious. He said, "So's mine".

In a broader sense, Becky and I have been fortunate to have the ability to find joy together every day, regardless of circumstances. In good times and bad, laughter is indeed the best medicine. Neither of us would allow the other to get down and stay down. That is not to say we were never down. Both of us were at times. But when you find yourself down, straighten up, stick your chest out, get your chin up, and find a way to have some fun. That's easier said than done and easier done with strong family support, with which we have always been blessed.

There was no way we were going to infect our lives and home with sadness, even during some of Collin's most difficult times. There was too much to be happy about. Becky and I have always maintained the same feelings we had when we first fell in love. Happiness reigned in our home from the beginning. Nothing was going to destroy that. Especially after reaching San Antonio, with Collin on a roll, doing better than he had in years, life was good!

Until Collin began his SIB at age 20, he had the personality to burn. He was a funny little guy who was lovable, very affectionate, and playfully bantered with us. Even during his worst times, he never lost his basic personality and ability to connect. Collin spent his last six years at his home in San Antonio Texas which was a giant step forward with mostly good days. Our family and Collin were truly blessed as Collin made progress far beyond our hopes and dreams.

Though this group home program was top-notch, during the six years of his residency, Collin managed to blind himself after about two years. Collin detached the retina in both eyes by unexpectedly and suddenly banging his head on the kitchen table. That wasn't the fault of the staff or anyone. As previously mentioned, a helmet had been tried at Abilene State School to protect him from this type risk. It was decided there was likely more risk to use the helmet than not.

At every instance, Collin found a way to thwart any effort to protect him if he chose to harm himself. It became a judgment call as to how to provide the best possible quality of life, with as much safety as possible, and within reasonable limits of restraint. A helmet not used, he blinded himself. Restraints necessary to protect him from "everything" seemed to be a likely worse choice than the risk of some injury.

How can that be comparatively evaluated? It can't be. There are stories of individuals fully restrained, in every conceivable manner, who found ways to do serious self-injury. Where is the quality of life if one can't do anything? You go with your best judgment and don't second guess yourself, lest you lose your mind.

Collin had banged his head on a table, and as blood pooled in his eyes, we rushed him to a doctor and eventually to the hospital emergency room. A doctor said he would be hospitalized and heavily sedated as an important first step. But as hours passed no one wanted to sign the admission papers. We were told that *Internal Medicine* wouldn't admit him because he had no internal issues. *Ophthalmology* wouldn't admit him because they feared he would injure himself. *Psychiatry* wouldn't admit him because Collin couldn't consent, even though I was his legal guardian. But, … they said they were working on it.

Collin had been there, strapped to a gurney, for more than eight hours. Only when "everybody" else in this ER had been treated, in the early morning hours, and after I threatened to invite the media, was Collin finally admitted. The next morning a physician suggested we move him to a more "suitable environment." When I asked what type of facility he deemed "suitable," he suggested a totally inappropriate setting.

Whether the setting was appropriate was of no concern to the hospital. Even though he was heavily sedated with family and group home attendant present, and unable to cause trouble, the doctors just wanted him OUT. They didn't get that done. A parent, guardian, or caregiver should never have to battle the system to receive appropriate care for a special-needs patient.

The attitudes on display within the hospital during this episode were in sharp contrast to the kindness and compassion of the ophthalmologist in a subsequent appointment. Unfortunately, the examination revealed that both of Collin's retinas had detached. Under normal circumstances, a detached retina can sometimes be repaired. But the inability to keep Collin still enough to heal negated that possibility. The result was total blindness. The ophthalmologist gave us his personal cell phone number with instructions to call him if we had further questions or concerns. Years later, Becky saw him in a medical facility hallway and had an opportunity to once again express our gratitude and appreciation for his kindness. We love that guy.

Approximately four years later, Becky and I were on our way to Lubbock, over five hours from San Antonio, and as we approached the outskirts of town, a very distraught Deanne called to let us know Collin was in the ER with a broken arm, and rather than admit him, the doctor planned to release him with only a soft straight cast. Deanne knew he would literally tear his arm off in that situation. I spoke with the attending ER doctor who hung up on me before I could explain why the soft cast was not sufficient. After going up the chain, I secured a reluctant acceptance of the hospital to allow Collin to stay until our arrival.

At about 2:30 a.m. we arrived back at the emergency room. After more discussions with hospital staff, we received a verbal commitment for Collin's admittance. For whatever their reasons, the orthopedic surgeon at the hospital would only do a soft cast. The soft cast was redone, apparently better positioned, and better secured. The hospital wouldn't honor their verbal commitment to admit Collin to the hospital. We gave up and took him back to the group home, only to find the arm bending above the cast. Unfortunately, the surgeon who did the second soft cast didn't manage to cover the break. Oh, … but he was close.

Finally, Collin was admitted to another hospital for 23 hours to reset the bone and better secure the soft cast. Even this admitting hospital initially limited Collin's stay to 23 hours. For some reason, the surgeon was adamant in ruling out surgery. Collin was sedated and taken for the procedure. The surgeon came running down the hall … Collin had a brand-new puncture wound that required surgery.

That was good news to me. Proper treatment was going to happen. A little later the surgeon came running down the hall again. The plates, pins, or other equipment necessary to perform the procedure were not available. This was in a major hospital on a Tuesday morning. The hospital had no way to obtain equipment to perform surgery on a broken arm? In any case, the surgery was rescheduled for the following Thursday. Although the surgeon told us the surgery went to perfection, the truth was that he had aspirated during surgery, which resulted in aspiration pneumonia, from which Collin never recovered.

Weeks after Collin passed, I was talking with an orthopedic surgeon about the situation. He said that a surgeon should never, under any circumstances, postpone surgery more than six hours following a puncture wound, if at all avoidable. Collin's surgeon, touted as one of the best, waited two days.

We never asked the caregiver what happened when Collin broke his arm. He was a kind soul and totally dedicated to Collin's care. We didn't want him to think we placed blame or questioned anything he had or had not done. Despite his 19 IQ, Collin understood leverage and how to use it better than most people. The accident could have happened with anybody in attendance. Regardless, the staff told us he blamed himself.

During Collin's hospitalization following aspiration, the caregiver was distraught and disappeared for a while. We were all extremely worried about this fine man. Only hours before Collin passed, late at night, the young man appeared in Collin's hospital room. He didn't say a word, just stood at Collin's side and stared at him for several minutes. As he left the room, we offered as much support to him as we could, trying not to infringe on his private moments. Some days afterward, everyone was relieved when he returned to work

Some of the nicest, most caring people we have ever met involved in Collin's care were hospital physicians and nurses. From some local family doctors, to Fort Worth Children's Hospital personnel and attending specialists, to Abilene State School physicians, and professionals in San Antonio, most dealt with Collin with competence, compassion, and humility. We love them for that.

However, as previously mentioned, issues arose with some hospitals, ER services, and some physicians. Whatever the reasoning or bias, some of these did not want to deal with an individual like Collin. The negative issues I have described above were not intended to be an indictment of any medical system or any group of physicians. But there were circumstances and moments when Collin was regarded as less important and someone that certain unnamed hospitals and surgeons were reluctant to properly treat.

Although I believe we may have had a pretty good case, we never contemplated or inquired about a lawsuit or complaint of any kind. If we had felt we could have harmed those responsible for the damage caused by neglect of our son, we would have sued them. That may not have been the best attitude, but it is true. However, the struggle would have been with the insurance company and likely without much consequence to those at fault.

I would bet the farm we would have been portrayed as parents, bitter because of a son's misfortune, trying to cash in. We needed to attempt to pull our lives back together, and not get distracted by a lengthy and uncertain legal battle to harm someone. Instead, we chose to let the higher powers of the universe deal with those guys. One of the doctors who had initially blocked the first requested hospitalization witnessed the result of his negligence. He left Collin's hospital room in tears.

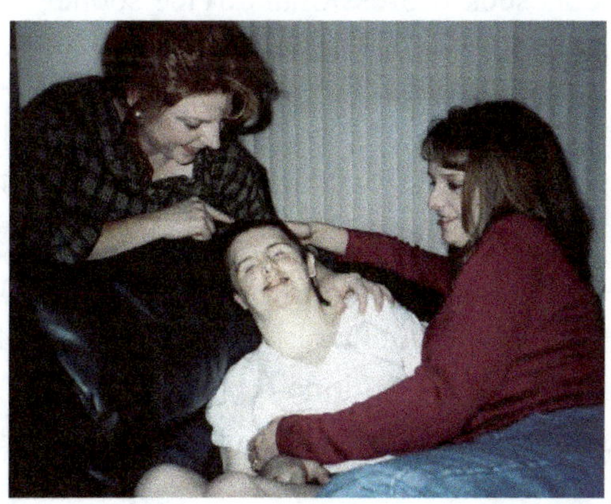

CHAPTER EIGHT
RETROSPECT, MIRACULOUS ENDING

Becky and I are certain we made many mistakes with Collin over the years. But what were the mistakes? At a given time, we always did what we believed was best for Collin based on our best judgment with the information we had. Given the same choices, we would probably repeat many of those same mistakes. 20/20 hindsight is only what we think an alternative result might have been. When you do all you can do, that is all you can do. Do we have regrets? Absolutely, but there is no reason to guilt ourselves for actions we thought were the best at the time.

I am almost convinced Collin was headed down the path he took regardless of anything we might have done differently, but there is no way to be certain. Knowing what we know now, we probably should have called in experts early on regarding his obsessive behavior. I recommend parents seek professional advice sooner rather than later. We were inclined to seek advice later, which was a mistake.

However, during one of my many conversations with State School mental health professionals, one of them explained to me that the system was full of lower-end IQ individuals who self-injured. He explained that when IQ is low enough, many will self-injure. He didn't elaborate further than that, but had I pursued that line of conversation, he would have probably mentioned other potential accompanying issues. It has been almost thirty years since that conversation.

If you search for information on self-injurious behavior (SIB) today, you will discover many factors that influence SIB. IQ, autism, general health, seizures, sometimes undetected, and many other factors combine to produce SIB, unique to the individual displaying the symptoms. There are still vast unknowns concerning SIB and universal treatment because of the nature of the beast. Many years of study have brought insight, but there is an enormous amount yet to be discovered.

From birth to death Collin's story is one of elation, to devastation, to unconditional love, to good times, to tough times, to tragedy, to triumph. Along the way, Collin unknowingly tossed pebbles in many ponds, with positive ripples still traveling.

Collin reached a mental age of something around 17-18 months. Even though he physically matured, he never advanced mentally past that of a toddler. We could interpret what pleased or displeased him by his actions. Although he couldn't talk, he could relate to and interact with people joyfully. Except during SIB episodes of his later years, he was always expecting to laugh about something.

All of his life Collin received the same level of attention from those around him that he did in his early years. The one that did the most, that Collin always looked to first, was Becky. There are no words to describe the constant efforts and sacrifices she made to enhance Collin's journey.

Someone (parents, sisters, family, friends, caregivers) was almost constantly talking to, redirecting, touching, jostling, and embracing him. He not only enjoyed the attention but expected it. One of his caregivers "affectionately" said he was a male chauvinist who thought all women were created for his benefit. Lots of truth there, but he expected the same amount of attention from men.

Describing interactions with a mental age of 17–18 month-old by means other than stories is difficult for me. Those interactions are generally insignificant, often funny, and almost constant. That's the typical type of interaction we had with Collin his entire life, even during his SIB. That said, many noteworthy stories resulted, a few of which have already been included. A few more will follow.

Collin had many nicknames. If I addressed him with a ridiculous-sounding name, and he laughed, he had a new nickname he would respond to. If he laughed at something, he heard it again and again. Funny sounds and tone of voice were keys. Collin and I gave each other high-fives quite often. Even when I spoke of many topics he didn't understand, he listened to me.

If he brought something from the cabinet or refrigerator, we knew what he wanted. He would instigate connection in many ways and loved to tease, e.g., look right and throw something past you to his left. Collin could throw very accurately. At the Special Olympics baseball throw event, he purposely threw the ball into the crowd rather than where he was being directed. He knew exactly what he was doing, but the opportunity to surprise was just too tempting to pass up.

The backs of Collin's ears were especially soft. Everybody familiar with him kissed and/or rubbed the back of his ears. Oh, how he liked that. A few typical photos have been provided. You will notice he was always smiling. Even in his worst days, he managed some smiles.

With his estimated IQ in the range of 19, Collin touched more people than most of us. **WITH ONE EXCEPTION, HE WAS NON-VERBAL**, but he could pull at those heartstrings. He bound our family together. Our little family of five, close relatives, and friends pulled together for Collin's sake. His presence inspired organizations to search for Special Needs people to serve and many individuals to look inward and ask "How can I help someone in need."

At a young age, Collin was king of the mountain from his perspective. He had no peer pressure. We joked that if he wanted a hammer and mirror to play with, we would give them to him. Our goal was to keep him happy and stimulate him as much as possible. In the family journeys to fulfill that goal, we made some very dear friends; friendships that have endured for decades. We still hear stories from years ago about how he used his shoes to communicate. When entering someone's house, if he removed his shoes and either threw or hid them, he intended to stay. On the other hand, if his shoes stayed on, chances were that we would be leaving with Collin in tow very soon.

From family and friends in Texas in the Afton area of his early years, to Stephenville, to Floydada, Abilene, and finally San Antonio, at each stop, there have been those who embraced and enjoyed Collin and had him in their prayers. During this journey, our little family had positive experiences and feelings that words cannot describe.

Collin's sisters never resented him, though they were shorted many times. They developed extraordinary gifts of compassion, tolerance, and generosity. Always in Collin's corner, they still tell beautiful and hilarious stories of their "little brother" to their children and others.

If Collin could have looked into the future across the universe and chosen two siblings, Deanne and Amy would have been the ones. It would have been impossible for two people to give more hugs and kisses than those two gave him. From small children, they understood he was allowed behaviors that we would not tolerate from them. When he emptied an entire gallon of milk across every cushion of the new sleeper sofa and ruined it, they understood why he didn't get scolded, when they would have been in big trouble. They knew they couldn't knock over the floor lamp, which he demolished frequently.

That said, we tried to keep him within some sort of parameters. I will never forget a particular day when Collin needed redirecting frequently. If it wasn't one thing it was two, and both Becky and I had been after him quite often that day. When one of us scolded one of the girls, Collin heard it and just cackled. Yep, it was about time they got their turn. He expressed his joy that somebody other than him was in trouble.

When he needed comfort and sympathy the girls were there. When he embarrassed them, at which he was quite efficient, they just loved him. To a fault, Deanne and Amy judged people on how they accepted their "little brother." They understood that people wouldn't always know what to expect from Collin or how to react but expected acceptance in the long run. If Collin embarrassed the girls, it was about what he had just done, not who he was. Even in their fragile teenage years, when they probably wanted to "kill" him a few times, they were always in his corner and never hesitated to introduce him.

As Collin began to have destructive behavior issues, the girls could calm and soothe him. Besides the many hugs and kisses that worked magic, they loved to rub lotion on his (always dry) feet, shave him when they could, and do whatever else made him happy and content.

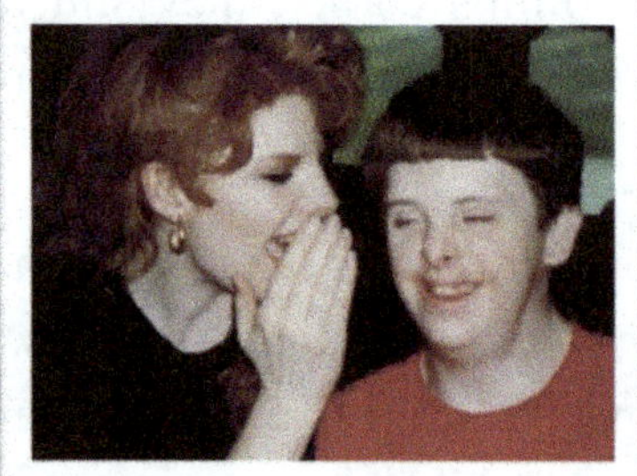

Proud of the girls' attitude, we had to temper their self-imposed feelings of obligation. I can't remember the specific conversation, but they informed Becky and me if something happened to us, they would take care of Collin, and we were not to worry. That was too heavy a load for them to even contemplate, much less commit to. Their future was at stake and there was no room for them to navigate their life's paths encumbered. I'm glad they brought those feelings up to us. We needed to assure them that wasn't going to be a responsibility of theirs. Collin would be taken care of without their assistance, regardless of the future. Becky and I had not anticipated the depths of the girls' sense of responsibility.

The following poem, accompanied by a photo of Collin in his baby blue suit, was written by Deanne after his passing. These words, from the depths of her heart and soul, best describe the core feelings and understandings of his sisters. Try to imagine what the world would look like with the universal perspective from which Collin viewed others.

BABY BLUE SUIT

You sit on my mantel in your baby blue suit

Blue eyes and long eyelashes
a precious, precious soul
a symbol of purity and innocence

Perfection
frozen in time for 32 years

You grew into a boy
then a man

And yet
Your innocence remains

Your childlike mind never understood
the ways of this world

Your heart never hardened
You never knew prejudice
Your love was unconditional

You have always been that little boy
in the baby blue suit

You will always sit on my mantel
and hold a special place in my heart

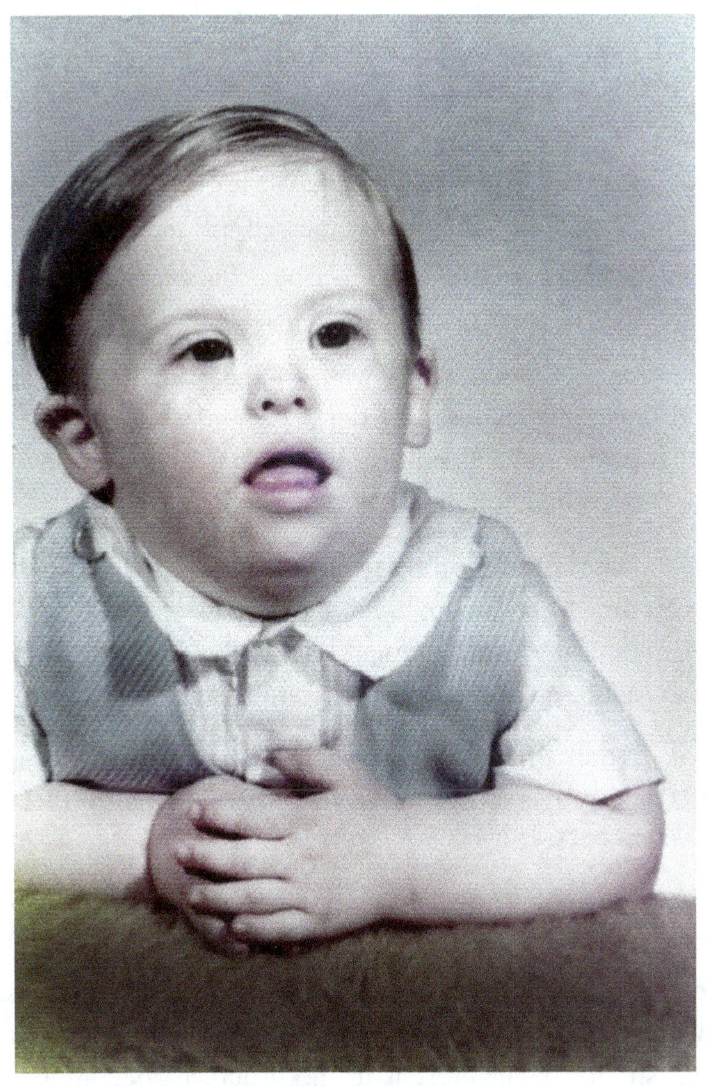

COLLIN HAD NEVER USED A SENTENCE IN CONVERSATION. HE COULDN'T. Moments before he passed, Collin pleasantly looked beyond us with his blind eyes and began speaking in conversational tones. It was like listening to one side of a foreign dialogue, in conversational structured sentences. Becky, her sister, Melanie, and I were in the room at the time. I didn't say anything about what I had seen and heard for a while but eventually brought it up to Becky. She had witnessed the same things as I had and drew the same conclusion.

Melanie said, "When I turned around, his eyes were open. They were focused, not on me, but he was looking over my right shoulder into the distance. It was just a matter of seconds, but at that moment, I knew that Collin saw someone or something....Then I knew he was gone....I believe in that moment he saw paradise".

I am convinced that Collin saw and communicated with the other side. I won't try to prove anything, but I know what I observed and believe Collin passed from torment to a glorious extension of eternal life almost before our eyes. I look forward to reuniting with him.

What greater gift could be received than to witness years of TRAGEDY for a loved one TRANSFORMED into TRIUMPH within MOMENTS?

Notwithstanding the difficulties of his last years, Collin had a very good life and brought great joy to all who knew and loved him. He freely gave and received much love. He could entertain himself for hours with the simplest of life's treasures. At the same time, he cherished simply being present in the group, participating with or entertaining others, or spending hours sitting quietly by someone he loved. There was not a single moment in his life in which he felt inferior to anyone.

Accompanying Collin on his journey opened our eyes and minds as we encountered some of the most beautiful, kind, and generous souls on this earth. We realized the sheer magnitude of people in more difficult circumstances than his, with little to no support network, and cemented our understanding of the strength of “pulling together”. Each of us can offer a shoulder to lean and cry on, a hand to lift someone up, or words of encouragement when the need arises.

Collin transformed our lives, and, as indicated in sweet posts, had a profound influence on many who knew him. Because of his ripples, others, including some who have never heard his name, have felt his influence. At the closing of his time on this earth, he had a **MARVELOUS AND TRIUMPHANT BEGINNING** that brings infinite peace to many of us.

May everyone who reads this receive a blessing in some way. Whether you draw any of the same perspectives or conclusions we have is irrelevant. Our hope is that we all pay more attention to the ripples we create every day. As we think of the influences of our life, let us take more care in the pebbles we cast. Collin had little to work with, yet his positive ripples are still rolling on. What will ours look like decades from now?

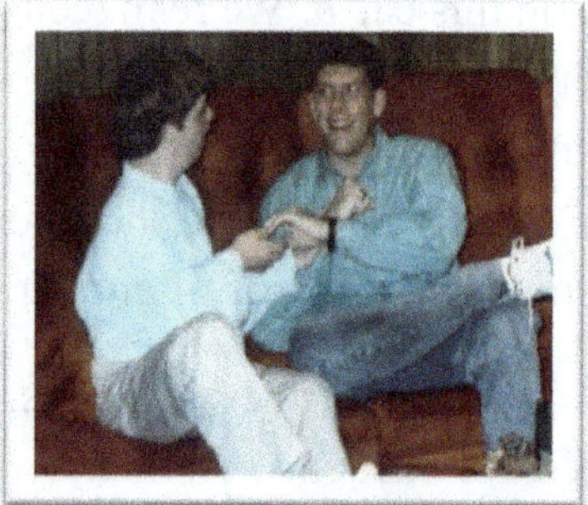

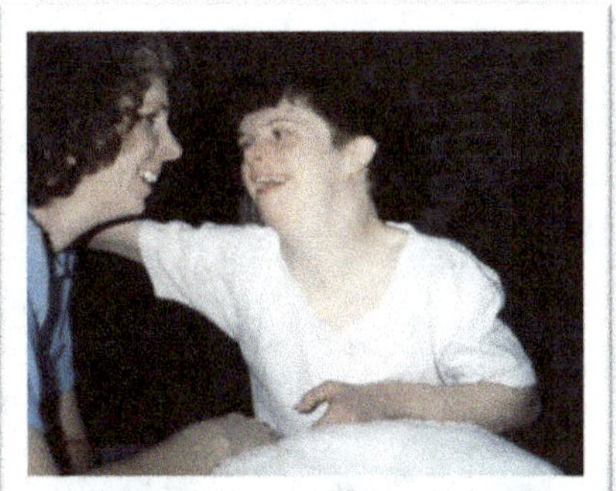

www.ingramcontent.com/pod-product-compliance
Lightning Source LLC
Chambersburg PA
CBHW050601160726
48003CB00002B/989

* 9 7 8 9 6 9 5 3 9 2 4 0 9 *